Grass Roots Politics

MORSHED ALAM

ISBN: 1497366321
ISBN-13: 978-1497366329

DEDICATION

I offer a special dedication to the following:

My late beloved father Abdus Samad Munshi and my late mother Aziunessa.

My brother, my idol, the late Sarwar Jhan Munshi and my late brother Monir Hossain. My mother and Monir Hossain were tragically killed in a car accident while on their way to the American Embassy to obtain a visa to the U.S. The accident broke our dreams of uniting my family.

My wife Saleha Khanam who made many sacrifices in order to help me to do all the things as an activist discussed in this book.

My three daughters: Nusrat Alam, Shaharin Alam, and Israt Alam.

And, finally, to all new Americans.

ACKNOWLEDGMENTS

A special thanks to my editor, Donald MacLaren, for his professional editing and rewriting, as well as to Bruce Chadwick, Ph.D. for being a very helpful editorial consultant.

MORSHED ALAM

CONTENTS

PREFACE

One of my goals in life has been to encourage new Americans, that is, immigrants to participate in the political system and civic clubs where they can learn how politics and activism work in the United States.

I believe this book will help to influence the immigrant community in a positive way by showing them that they can learn to overcome the struggles they face as new Americans; they can learn from their hardships; they can learn that the American system can work for them; they can learn that their involvement in American society is very critical to them personally and their involvement will help others to have new respect for them and their children.

As an immigrant who arrived in America twenty-five years ago, I have come to learn things about American politics that a lot of natural born Americans do not know. I continue to learn every minute of every day and I'm teaching new immigrants and natural born Americans as often as possible. In this book, I want to motivate others to do more in their communities and for this great country—America.

INTRODUCTION

1957

I was born in a village called Balakhal, then part of East Pakistan. The name of my house was called the Munshi family, a very famous and renowned family involved in politics. One of my cousins, Dr. Abdus Satter, distinguished himself in politics by becoming a member of Parliament in 1970-1971 during the liberation war, and afterwards he was re-elected in 1974 to the Bangladesh Parliament when the country became independent from Pakistan.

My father, a small businessman and farmer in the southern part of the country, had five sons and he managed to provide us with a healthy, happy life.

I attended elementary school in the neighboring village. At that time, parents who had a little money or were better off could afford to send their children to school.

I grew up loving politics, probably because political and civic issues were frequently discussed in our home. My personal awareness of "politics" came as I learned to run for student government positions and I discovered my fellow students voted for me: in third grade I was the class captain; in sixth grade I was the assistant general secretary of the student council; in ninth grade, I was the general secretary of the Student League. The Student League used to organize a student movement that represented student rights, education rights, and cultural rights in what would become known as Bangladesh.

After I graduated from Uchangha Primary School, I went on to high school. In high school, I became the assistant general secretary of the district of the Movement Against Pakistan Culture. Pakistan had tried to implement its language and impose its culture on the Bangladeshi people. Our student movement took the initiative to oppose this movement. I believed that we in Bangladesh did not want to lose our identity to Pakistan. Our student opposition inspired others, which in turn, created a national movement against Pakistan's intentions of absorbing the Bangladesh people. As a ninth grader and the secretary general of the local district, I found myself thrust into a national independence movement to establish a new government to protect our own culture and language.

I found a lot of my inspiration through my older brother, Mr. Sarwar Jhan, because he had become the Head Master (principal) of a school and then a School Inspector (Superintendent of the School Board). My older brother became the idol in my life, the one who got me thinking about civic involvement and politics. Because of his inspiration, I became the activist that I am today. He certainly inspired me to get a better education. In addition, I have to give credit to my family relatives, including my cousins, who were all very educated and involved in their communities.

Between 1970 and 1971, a liberation struggle had begun against Pakistan. The Bangladesh people had their own army of what we called Freedom Fighters. My involvement with the Freedom Fighters was to supply them with food and to relay information to them as a courier. As a high school student, I did not carry a weapon or kill any Pakistani soldiers who were trying to maintain control, but my discreet role as a courier, informer, and organizer played an important role in our fight for freedom. I had to move around to different locations quickly without drawing attention to myself, so I learned how to cross the streets without being detected and how to move between the many locations of the Freedom Fighters without being caught.

Fighting did take place in my own village between the Pakistan army and the Freedom Fighters, resulting in many people killed and about 300 houses burned during the local fighting.

Near my house was the headquarters of our local district in Hajigonj. In 1972, I became the secretary general of my Student League district, representing about twenty-five thousand students at that time.

By the time I graduated from Balakhal High School, I had gained notoriety as a famous student leader in my district because of my involvement in the liberation causes.

Inspired by my older brother, I went on after high school to attend Chandpur College, a two-year college which had an enrollment of about 15,000 students. Getting to college every day required a lot of perseverance. I used to travel 24 miles every day, requiring me to start out by walking two miles to the train station, then riding the train twelve miles to the school, and making a final trek of a mile and a half to the college. If anyone asked me how it was getting to school, I had one answer, "It was very hard."

After graduating from the college, I had the opportunity to go to the famous Dhaka University, situated in the Bangladesh capitol of Dhaka. The university had been established in 1902 and had gained enough of a reputation to be called the "Oxford of the East." Since the university was about 100 miles north of my home, commuting was out of the question. I lived at one of the halls (dormitories) named after a very educated professor (Dr. Mohammad Shahidullaha) who is said to have known how to read, write, and speak in 18 languages.

While attending Dhaka University, I became a popular student leader. I was elected to be the assistant general secretary of the Dhaka University Student League, part of the central committee of the Bangladesh Student

League with over 10 million members. Eventually, I was the Foreign Affairs Secretary and the Press Secretary of this very prestigious organization. The Student League was instrumental in spearheading the movement against Pakistan and in helping to establish the democratic independence of Bangladesh.

The Bangladesh Student League was founded by Sheik Mujibur Rahman, who is now referred to as the father of Bangladesh. Soon after I enrolled in Dhaka University, Sheik Mujibur was assassinated by those in the Bangladesh Army who sided with Pakistan and who did not believe in Bangladesh achieving freedom. Sheik Mujibur, along with twenty-three members of his family and four powerful leaders of independence, were assassinated by some miscreants in the name of the army.

The sixteen Student League leaders started organizing a movement against all the killings and the oppression. After August 15, 1975, we started working for democracy because a small group in the army established a military regime that halted the movement for democracy in Bangladesh. The military leaders under General Ziawur Rahman suspended the constitution and all the democratic activities and turned Bangladesh into a dictatorship.

As leaders of the Student League, we said what he did was wrong and that he could not suspend democracy. We organized students, labor forces, farmers, and masses of people throughout the country. We had many demonstrations and uprisings of all the professional groups. A lot of people were beaten. Even I was beaten while in Dhaka University by General Rahman's police. I was forced into hiding and when I traveled to the demonstrations I would be disguised. I moved discreetly in the crowds at the meetings so the police would not get me. However, I remained as an involved, committed leader organizing the demonstrations and committed to establishing freedom based on democracy for the people.

I went to every district and sub-district in my country, including all the cities. While the organization paid for the traveling, I had to do a lot of sacrificing for the cause of freedom and democracy: never walking the

5

streets freely, but always moving around in disguise; organizing the student demonstrations at the risk of my own imprisonment; organizing workers' strikes around the country; and organizing all kinds of events and rallies for the cause of freedom.

I do not know whether that I or any of the other Student League leaders were put on an arrest list. However, if we were caught by the army, I believe we would certainly have spent years in prison and would have received serious beatings. While helping at one local election in 1978, I remember the Army soldiers coming there and beating the people, so we constantly faced beatings and the threat of imprisonment without any constitutional rights.

Finally in 1979, the military leaders who had established themselves to rule Bangladesh after it had become independent were forced to recognize the will of the people and so they re-established Parliament. I am proud that I was part of establishing democracy in Bangladesh. After about a five-year struggle, the Army generals realized that they could not stop us or keep us from establishing democracy. We had been telling the people all those years that democracy could not be suspended. We claimed freedom as one of our human rights by saying, "Democracy is the right of the individual!" By 1980, democracy was slowly restored through a new Parliament in Bangladesh.

But the fighting with Pakistan and the generals took a terrible toll. It is said that three million people were killed during our Bangladesh Liberation War in 1970 and about 500,000 women were tortured or raped. The people sacrificed their lives, their homes, and themselves in order to establish democracy and human rights in their country.

As students, we were supporting and helping our parents who had formed The Awami League whose goal was to fight for democracy in Bangladesh.

By 1978, I received my Bachelor's degree with honors, specializing in Soil Science.

Separate from my formal education and through my association with others fighting for freedom and democracy, I had come to learn some unique lessons about the grassroots techniques of organizing demonstrations and galvanizing the people to stand up against political dictatorships.

During this time, I continued my study of soil science, acquiring a master's degree in 1980. The tuition was paid for by a scholarship (75%) and my family's help (25%). I received my Master's degree rather quickly. Another major change took place in my life in September 21, 1980 when I married Saleha, who was then finishing her Bachelor degree at Dhaka University in home economics.

I like to say that I had an excellent education by being very involved with both the new political leaders and the intellectual, academic leaders of my country. By fighting for freedom, I came to understand and participate in the total political system of my former native Bangladesh.

On January 1, 1984, I moved to the United States as an immigrant with my wife.
When I came to the United States, politics in general was not new to me
.

While in high school, we used our native language. English became my second language while in the college and university because all the classes were taught in English. So, coming to America and speaking English was not an immediate problem as it can be for some immigrants. Of course, learning English in a foreign country and learning to speak the slangs and idioms in American English required a lot more practice of English.

Once the Army came into power as a dictatorship, I did not see any opportunities for myself in my country. I felt I could do better and contribute better to my family and country if I went abroad, specifically by going to America. Although the Army generals gradually relinquished their power to a new Parliament, I still believed America would be my better choice. Maybe in the back of my mind I worried that another dictator would come along and try to dissolve Parliament again, and so a fight for a new democracy would have to be waged once again. The fragile, unpredictable democracy of Bangladesh was not the political environment where Saleha and I wanted to raise our children.

My brother-in-law, Mr. Awlad Hossain Khan, had already come to the U.S. as a chemist and was working on Long Island, New York. He willingly sponsored my wife and me. My science background was not of particular help getting me in. I was in the fifth preference Visa system. Since a sister could automatically bring her family relatives, I managed to emigrate to the U.S. through our family connections.

My first job in the U.S. was working as a lab technician for Duramed, a pharmaceutical company in Westbury, Long Island, so we set up our home in Levittown, Long Island.

By 1985, some changes were taking place in our lives: our first daughter, Nusrat Alam, had been born and we moved to Queens Village, a neighborhood in Queens, one of the five boroughs of New York City. One edge of Queens bordered the East River, facing Manhattan, while the section where we had moved was closer to JFK International Airport.

I considered right away Queens Village my new home in the United States. With a sense of "home," I wanted to become involved with the political-civic life of this southern part of Queens.

The first thing I did was to organize our Bangladesh community. I knew how to make connections. I became a member of the Bangladesh Society of New York, which had a wider net of members in what was called the tri-state area, including New Jersey, New York, and Connecticut. For reasons of familiarity and social networking, I preferred organizing our Bangladesh people, so I organized the Bangladesh Awami League Chapter in New York.

After that, I began to learn how to be part of the local civic associations and the local Democratic Party. I applied for citizenship because I could not participate in politics without being a citizen. By

8

October, 1989, I can proudly say that I realized one of my dreams: I became a U.S. Citizen.

In 1990 and with my citizenship established, I joined the Eastern Queens Democratic Club. I became one of the rising local political stars: a member of the board; a community liaison; Vice President; and Chairman of the Board of Directors. Slowly, I was getting involved in local American politics with the hope of doing greater things later on.

In 1992, I made a career move and started working for New York City as a chemist. As a city employee, I was introduced to the new world of union politics, so I became a member of Local 375 of the AFL-CIO and elected delegate to Local 375.

During this time, I enjoyed absorbing all I could about local politics and union politics. I felt I was quickly becoming immersed in American civic, political, and union causes.

In 1994, a new movement had begun growing against immigrants. Proposition 187 in California proposed an anti-immigrant agenda with the most specific issues being that there would be no health care for illegal immigrants and the children of the illegals could not attend public school.

Proposition 187 galvanized me into taking action. I took a strong stand against that proposition by organizing nationwide groups to campaign against it and by speaking against the proposition in New York State. State Senator Frank Padavan (Republican) had written an anti-immigrant book, *Claiming Our Shore*. He was riding the anti-immigrant sentiment at the time, while I vehemently opposed. Since Padavan was a politician, I was motivated to build a movement against him. My goal was to build a multi-ethnic, multi-religious, and multi-color coalition that would vote against him. I wanted to show the politicians that immigrants were a political power to be courted and not to be treated as second-class citizens.

9

By 1996, I had formed a coalition of different groups, a very wide variety of ethnic groups—Chinese, Korean, West Indies, Black, Hispanic, Jewish, Eastern European. I traveled around to all the different communities to get them organized. And besides the ethnic groups, I involved myself in groups representing Human Rights and Women's Rights.

Having experience with the Democratic Party in Queens, I decided to form my own political club made up of immigrants. I called it the New American Democratic Club.

I can proudly say that my achievements were reported in *Newsday* when the newspaper chose me as the "Everday Hero," a special recognition in the Sunday edition of the paper recognizing one Queens resident who has made significant contributions to making Queens better (May 19, 2002). Although I may be called a hero, I have gone through my share of struggles too.

My story in this book is about what happened in my union, civic, and political struggles in New York City.

CHAPTER 1

GRASS ROOTS POLITICS

Everyone, including my fellow South Asians, should pay close attention to the politics in their area. Issues that affect the quality of our lives are decided everyday by people within and outside our neighborhoods. Since that is a fact of life, let us resolve to take some action to be in charge of our destinies, at least as far as politics is concerned, rather than waiting for things to happen to us. Part of my message is to encourage people to be active politically and in civic affairs.

When referring to immigrants, I may prefer to use "we" because I, too, am an immigrant, although I am now more established after being in the United States for more than twenty years. My story may be reduced to this: I got involved in my community. Many people came to know me for my civic-political-human rights concerns and activities.

Of course, you are not obligated to run for public office to show that you are taking part in the government decisions that affect your lives. Common sense and a far-sighted view of the future, however, tells me that information is power and when it comes to asking things from the government, we need the information (power) to know what to ask and

11

from whom to ask! We must learn who is likely to support us or to listen to
our requests and who is not, enabling us to act or plan accordingly. Even
though some of us do not like to get involved, we are part of American
society and that requires from us a sense of responsibility. I challenge new
Americans and all Americans to act **as part** of their community, instead of
setting themselves **apart** from the mainstream.

In New York City, South Asians, for example, have many
opportunities and resources to help them get involved in the civic and
political lives of their neighborhoods. Involvement is synonymous with
improvements. The improvements that you want to see for your
neighborhood or city to the benefit of you and your children comes through
your involvement. In the cities, block associations of neighbors and
residents work to improve the conditions of their blocks and look out for
each other. Civic associations perform similarly to block associations,
except over a larger area and also address more issues, including public
policy and legislation. Tenant groups act similarly in apartment buildings
and complexes, and also interact with landlords and government agencies
for better conditions. Chambers of commerce and local merchants or
professional associations provide forums for merchants and professionals
to work with their colleagues on issues of mutual concern. Issue-oriented
groups address particular issues of concern, such as the treatment of
immigrants, health care, pollution, and discrimination. Labor unions allow
new Americans workers to join with others for fair working conditions and
may provide an entrance into political life, given the political activity by
many labor unions.

Civic or neighborhood associations (they are known by many names
in New York City) deserve particular attention. Civic associations bring
together neighbors from different blocks in a geographic area to monitor
the delivery of public services, obtain and distribute information about
changes in laws and public services to local residents, and advocate for
their concerns with public officials and private interests. These associations
are usually non-partisan, which only adds to their strength in this case
because local elected officials know that these groups tend to be fairly
representative of local unions and the union members are likelier to vote

and act than non-members who live in the same neighborhood. In other words, politicians pay attention to civic groups because members tend to be doers (at least they attend meetings and join a group) and thus, politicians can expect a reaction (often a group reaction) to their acts, specifically in getting people's votes.

The Charter of New York City provides people of all ethnicities with opportunities to express their opinions, learn about local developments, and participate in some fashion at the local level. The 59 Community Boards in New York City can provide an opportunity for participation.

Community Boards exist to advise the city government on various issues, particularly zoning and land use, budget, and quality of life concerns. While they are without legislative power, the Community Boards serve as local forums to discuss local needs and express the people's opinions to government agencies and representatives of elected officials and interest groups in areas covered by Community Boards. New York is not the only municipality to have such bodies; Washington, D.C. has its Advisory Neighborhood Commissions.

For large cities, these bodies offer a way to learn and get involved without having to raise funds for campaigns. In smaller cities, towns, and villages, new American residents should attend meetings of local boards or councils (they are usually public) to learn and eventually express themselves (when there are opportunities to do so at these meetings).

In New York City, a Community Board has up to 50 members, who serve renewable two-year terms. Members are appointed by the Borough President (New York City is composed of five "boroughs," or counties), half of these appointments must be on the advice of local City Councilmen in the area represented by the particular Community Board. Each Community Board elects its Chairperson and officers and hires a District Manager and staff to monitor and coordinate the delivery of public services and resolve complaints or questions about local services from residents. Community Boards usually meet once a month, not counting committee meetings.

In New York City, it is interesting to note two facts about U.S. Citizenship related to the Community Boards: (1) citizenship is **not** required for appointment to Community Boards, and (2) citizenship is not required to speak or ask questions during the public speaking time of Community Board meetings, or to even attend them! Thus, in areas of high immigrant populations, there is really no reason why immigrants should not try to obtain some representation on Community Boards. Such representation will not be merely given, it must be sought through establishing a presence in the community and relations with people who influence the selection of members. In other words, immigrants must get involved like everyone else.

Another vehicle that deserves discussion are the political party clubs. In the 2008, the following parties are listed on the ballot: Democratic, Republican, Independence, Conservative, Working Families, Socialist Workers, Socialism & Liberation, Green, Libertarian, and Populist. The two major parties, Democratic and Republican, have clubs located in every county to organize their members, support their candidates, and spread their message. The smaller parties have not so many clubs, but can play important roles in areas where they are strong. Given that most elected officials in New York are elected as candidates of political parties, political party clubs are excellent places to establish relationships with people who think like us, to support or oppose issues or candidates, and to learn the operations of campaigns.

These clubs work to get out the vote on primary and election days, and provide opportunities to communicate with local officials at meetings and events. At these clubs, votes and money matter. Thus, immigrants should use their resources within the law to gain clout and respect from local decisionmakers and even become part of groups that make decisions affecting their daily lives. We should also establish ties with all political forces that are not hostile to us so that we may be able to deal with whomever is in power.

Education is a subject of primary importance to immigrants. While it is good that our parents are interested in getting our children the best education possible, one approach is not sufficiently pursued by our people: Involvement in Parent-Teachers Association and School Board elections. Until recently in New York City, the 32 local Community School Boards (which operated under one central Board of Education) controlled budgets in the millions of dollars, employment, curriculum, and other facets of the public education of our children from kindergarten to eighth grade. In other words, most immigrants in New York City have left their children to the decisions of others as far as their educational future was concerned and no one like us making those decisions!

Each Community School Board has nine seats, which are filled by non-partisan elections every three years. The method of election, the single-transferable vote, is such that minorities like South Asians have a chance of electing someone in districts where our numbers are sufficiently concentrated. But even where our numbers are lower, we should form coalitions to make ourselves heard! That is how I won election to the School Board myself.

When I ran for the School Board in 1996, very few people expected me to win. After all, no South Asian had been elected to any public office before in New York City and our concentration in my district (District 29) was not so evident to local political observers. But after evaluating factors and possibilities to win a seat, I concluded that victory lay in forming a coalition with like-minded people of different groups in my community School District. I also made sure to learn New York's rigorous rules on getting on the ballot.

Community School District 29 is located in southeastern Queens, including the neighborhoods of Jamaica Estates, Jamaica Hill, part of Jamaica, Hollis, Hollis Park Gardens, Holliswood, Queens Village, part of Bellerose, Cambria Heights, St. Albans, Laurelton Springfield Gardens, Rosedale, and Rosedale Gardens. About 300,000 people live in this district, which also contains J.F.K. International Airport and Belmont Race Track, and 27,000 of our district's children attend 28 elementary and intermediate schools. About two-thirds of District 29's population is African-American, with Whites, Hispanics, and Asians sharing the rest. The conditions did not seem auspicious for my campaign.

Nevertheless, I came to the School Board election campaign with a name and reputation from years of involvement in numerous party, interest groups (and campaign experience), civic and professional organizations, from which I made many contacts, alliances, and friendships I could use to build a base, which at first I did not appear to have. While the Reverend Jesse Jackson may have called his presidential campaign a "Rainbow Coalition," my effort was backed by a mini-Rainbow Coalition that was dazzling in its diversity. Consider that my campaign manager, Kevin Wong, is Chinese-American, his assistant, John Knight, is Irish-American, my Campaign Chairman, Arthur F. Rojas, Esq. is Hispanic, and my Campaign Vice-Chairman, Marc Haken, is Jewish!

Reaching beyond race and ethnicity, my supporters reflected years of experience and support from various professional, civic, religious, and political organizations that spanned the spectrum locally and objectively. For example, Mr. Rojas, my Campaign Chairman, is a long-time friend who had contemplated running for the School Board before switching to support me. In doing so, he lent me his connections to leaders of civic associations (he was President of the Queens Village Civic Association at the time), local activists of political parties (we reached out to every party on the ballot except for Freedom), and Hispanic groups. At the same time, Chet Szarejko, a mentor and Democratic District Leader in eastern Queens, provided me with advice and connections to the Democratic Party. I also contacted activists of other parties: John Cronin (Queens County leader of the Right-to-Life Party) and Richard Burns (local Republican activist). Critical support from the Black community came from civic activists such as Leana Norton (President, Our Neighborhood Improvement Association) and parent leaders such as Glynis Harrison (President, P.T.A. of P.S. 131 in Jamaica Estates). My Asian compatriots energetically registered to vote and enlisted support from a variety of sources, including leaders of mandirs and mosques!

16

Together, we were able to obtain more signatures than any other candidate in District 29 and presented our petitions to comply with the Education Law and Election Law to avoid challenges. Although this process was extremely arduous and stressful, it provided valuable practice to my colleagues and me and we made it onto the ballot. Many times candidates in New York lose not because they fail to win enough votes, but due to problems with New York's intricate ballot access requirements.

I was able to attract support from most parts of the political spectrum by emphasizing my concerns as a parent and taxpayer and years of community activity. In addition, while my belief in traditional morality and family values helped me win support from more conservative civic and political leaders, my activism in labor and immigrant issues helped me reach out to more progressive forces, such as labor unions.

Our "omni-directional" strategy, designed in large part by Mr. Rojas and executed by Messrs. Kwong, Knight, and Haken, and supported by a host of volunteers from within and outside District 29 worked beyond our wildest expectations. I was elected to School Board 29 in May 1996 with the highest number of votes of any of the candidates, even out-polling Claudette Webb, the incumbent President of the Board!

My volume of votes helped propel my two colleagues on my slate: a Black incumbent (Thelma V. Prescott) and the first Colombian-American elected to public office in New York City (Rosa E. Browne) into office as well. My happiness was further increased weeks later with news that my friend Sachi G. Dastidar, Ph.D., survived a recount to win a School Board seat in Community School District 26 (northeastern Queens), thus doubling our South Asian representation in New York City's Community School Boards.

After being sworn in July 1, I was elected Treasurer of the School Board by my colleagues and I approached my duties with vigor. I have kept my pledge to visit neighborhood groups and parents in my region of the district and to increase respect for the District's geographical and ethnic diversity. Furthermore, I have been able to contribute our values to decisions made at the School Board. For example, I was a co-sponsor of a moment of reflection to start the school day in District 29, as well as securing increased programming and attention to Asian cultures.

In two years, the voters of District 29 will judge me once again on my performance as a School Board member. My path to office and my past involvement shows that South Asians can establish a constructive and effective presence in the civic and political lives in their communities. The way to meaningful participation does not require us to surrender our identities or lose our values. We can do well for ourselves and good for American society by swimming **in** the mainstream instead of staying apart from the mainstream and passively watching others move ahead.

Used by permission from the Chief-Leader Newspaper

November 13, 1998

UNION OFFICIAL SEES POLITICS UP CLOSE

BY MARK DALY

It was lunchtime on Election Day, and campaigners for Morshed Alam, the Democratic candidate for State Senate in northeast Queens, had met up at their usual rendezvous—the basement of Mr. Alam's Jamaica Estates home.

With maps of the 11th Senate District decorating the otherwise bare walls of the cramped quarters, volunteers ducked out of range of the fax machines and cell phones in the main room to linger over a side table stacked with donuts and pastries. The campaign's manager, Arthur F. Rojas, gave final instructions to a worried-looking volunteer who would be observing vote-tallying at a polling site that night.

'Forget the Other Guys'

"For each race, they're going to announce the figures," the Queens attorney explained, striking his palm to drive each point home. "I don't care about eh Governor's race, I don't care about the Attorney General's race, I don't care about the other Senate race—Schumer or D'Amato. The only race I care about is 'For State Senate: Morshed Alam.'"

Pausing to greet a visitor, Mr. Rojas pointed to the extremely low ceiling. "We call it the Viet Cong Campaign Headquarters," he said with a grin.

Underground allusions fir the mood of the insurgent campaign of Mr. Alam, a Chemist at the New York City Department of Environmental Protection and a chapter president at the Civil Service Technical Guild Local 375 of District Council 37.

In choosing to run his first campaign for state office against Queens Republican Frank Padavan, an incumbent completing his 25th year in Albany, Mr. Alam said he faced twin challenges of union leaders more comfortable with a familiar face and a country Democratic organization reluctant to make waves.

And while he didn't consider it an obstacle, Mr. Alam also had less time to match the political education of his experienced rival. A U.S. Resident for 14 years and a citizen for nine, the Bangladesh-born Mr. Alam viewed his campaign as a grand American civics lesson as well as a step toward his life's ambition.

"Today I get my Ph.D. in politics," Mr. Alam mused earlier that morning, taking a break from touring polling places to sip coffee at a fast-food restaurant. "Without running for a position, nobody can really understand the legislative process. Without actually running, it's hard to learn the whole thing."

Beginning in the third grade, when he ran for class president, Mr. Alam has sought out a political career. As a college student in Dacha, Bangladesh's capital, he headed a student group and toured the country as an organizer for education initiatives and other public-interest measures.

Though a cousin got himself elected to the nation's Parliament, Mr. Alam went down a different road, emigrating to New York with his wife, Saleha, to start a family that now includes three daughters. He entered city service in 1992 after working for a pharmaceutical company, and almost immediately began serving in union offices.

Stuck on Job List

"I wanted to join the labor movement and I wanted to see government from the inside," Mr. Alam said. His time with the city has been both rewarding and dispiriting, he added, noting he has been waiting almost four years to be selected off a promotion list to replace the provisional Assistant Chemists in his DEP division, which monitors the city's water supply.

Mr. Alam ran and won a campaign for a community school board seat in 1996, but his greatest hurdle in the State Senate race was, in his words, "building our own organization." County Democrats refused to nominate him, he said, forcing him to gather 1,200 signatures on his own to get on the party ballot.

"If the party doesn't support you, you're in trouble," Mr. Alam said, ticking off the lesson of the race. "And if somebody challenges your signatures, you're in trouble."

Seeking to share the lessons of the campaign trial, Mr. Alam enlisted the help of other "new Americans" in the diverse 11th District through a political club he founded in 1996. The club registered hundreds of new voters among the district's newly minted citizens, and organized more than 200 volunteers for the petitioning drive.

Campaign chairman Marc Haken—a retired city Teacher, veteran labor organizer and independent-minded Queens Democratic Party man—nodded in approval.

"What is it in Spanish—saber es poder? Political knowledge is power," Mr. Haken said. After the election, a lot of these people will be moving on to the year 2000, when the City Council seats open up."

In the general election, Local 375 backed Mr. Alam with an endorsement from President Roy Commer and a $1,000 campaign donation, but District Council 37, the United Federation of Teachers and the Central Labor Council all told him they would favor Mr. Padavan, Mr. Alam said.

He later derided the unions as "hypocrites."

"They didn't think I had a chance," Mr. Alam said. "They should think about that. I grew up middle-class, but I'm part of the labor movement too. I believe there should be job protection and better benefits. I'm in favor of all labor issues."

Outspent nearly two to one by an entrenched incumbent, Mr. Alam's leap to state office fell short. He was elated, however, by unofficial tallies that showed him getting above 40 percent of the vote.

"I think I proved that without any help, I can run any kind of campaign. In about a month I'll get together with my supporters," he said, and figure out what to run for next.

𝕿𝖍𝖊 𝕹𝖊𝖜 𝖄𝖔𝖗𝖐 𝕿𝖎𝖒𝖊𝖘
nytimes.com

Reprinted by permission from The New York Times

December 28, 1999

Immigrant Diversity Slows Traditional Political Climb

BY JAMES DAO

As a teenager, Morshed Alam dodged enemy soldiers to deliver food to Bangladeshi independence fighters. And as a student at Dhaka University in the mid-1970's, he endured police beatings to organize pro-democracy demonstrations against the newly formed nation's military regime.

So it is hardly surprising that Mr. Alam dived headlong into American politics soon after immigrating to Queens 15 years ago. In 1996, he became the first Bangladeshi on a New York City community school board. In 1998, he challenged an entrenched Republican state senator. And when the county Democratic organization opposed his candidacy, he built his own insurgent political club.

"Politics is the same everywhere in the world," said Mr. Alam, who lost the 1998 race but plans to run again next year. "Nobody wants to give up their power. But times are changing."

Ambitious and impatient, sour on local Democrats but enthusiastic about democracy, Mr. Alam is a prime example of a new breed of immigrant politicians from Asia, the West Indies and Latin America who are beginning to take their places at the city's table of power, just as Italian and East European Jewish immigrants did 90 years ago.

Some, like Mr. Alam, are rebelling against established politicians. Others are rebuilding dying political clubs. Still others are entering politics the old-fashioned way by running for ground-floor offices, like a spot on

23

the school board, competing in races that often draw yawns from native-born politicians.

They are scoring small but significant successes. Dominicans control the Democratic clubs of Washington Heights. Asian-Americans hold five elected judicial positions and 15 seats on nine different school boards. And there are now eight people of West Indian descent in the City Council and State Legislature.

But the new immigrants have yet to reach the higher rungs of the city's political ladder. No Asian-Americans, West Indians or Latin Americans in New York City are Democratic county leaders, members of Congress or strong contenders for citywide office. Oddly enough, the thing they are celebrated for, their extraordinary diversity, has weakened their political strength.

Today's immigrants come from more countries and speak more languages than the last great wave of European immigrants. They are more economically varied, with highly educated and skilled people among their ranks. And more than their predecessors, they are eschewing homogeneous enclaves, scattering to neighborhoods across the city.

Fractured and dispersed, they have proved more difficult to unite into political movements. In New York, no group approaches the influence of Cuban immigrants in Miami, Mexican immigrants in San Antonio or even Asian-Americans in San Francisco, whose political power has been amplified by their more concentrated numbers.

"There hasn't been a citywide candidate who can jell the immigrants, partly because it is such a diverse community," said John Mollenkopf, a professor of history at the City University of New York.

But the city's political landscape is changing in ways that could catapult more immigrant politicians into office. In 2001, term limits will force 36 of the 51 City Council members from office. Presented with that historic opportunity, political analysts predict, large numbers of immigrants will be registering voters and building organizations -- trying to rouse communities many veteran politicians once felt safe to ignore.

And the immigrants will be there for the rousing. Since 1996, record numbers have applied for citizenship, spurred by Congress's decision to end welfare benefits for certain non citizens and by the advent of dual citizenship in countries like the Dominican Republic and Colombia, which send large numbers of immigrants to America.

Mr. Alam, a cheerful, rail-thin man of 42 who is an environmental chemist for the city, is hoping to ride that wave to victory.

Last year, he challenged State Senator Frank Padavan, a 13-term Republican who had made an issue of the cost of social services for immigrants. When the Queens Democratic Party refused to support Mr. Alam, he recruited immigrants into his own organization, the New American Democratic Club. With a shoestring budget and little campaign experience, they knocked on doors, gave out literature and helped him win 41 percent of the vote.

A recent meeting of the club showed it to be as kaleidoscopic as the city itself. Among the 35 people eating chicken tikka and basmati rice at Mr. Alam's house in Jamaica were school board members from Korea and Taiwan; an Indian dentist and Pakistani professor; Roman Catholics from Colombia and Black Muslims from Brooklyn.

Their accents were as varied as their faces. They wore business suits, saris and flowing white robes. But they could clearly agree on one thing: it was time to have a voice, perhaps many, in American politics.
"We have to show them we belong," Elizabeth Aivars, a Venezuelan immigrant, told the group. "This is a political organization. We're not embarrassed to say that."

Getting Noticed
Jews and Italians Show the Way
On a November morning in 1914, hundreds of Jewish immigrants gathered along East Broadway in the chill before dawn, singing, dancing and hoping to catch a glimpse of their hero: Meyer London, a Socialist Party leader who had just been elected to Congress from the Lower East Side.

To those immigrants, Mr. London's election was a watershed. He was one of them, a new American who had come from Russia as a youth, the son of a print shop owner, a lawyer for garment workers. His election seemed to validate their yearnings for political influence and economic security.

Two years later, the city's Italian immigrant community elected its first member of Congress, Fiorello H. La Guardia. (Actually, La Guardia could claim a dual heritage; his father was Italian, his mother, Jewish. And in 1933, he was able to build a multi-ethnic, multi party coalition to become mayor, the first Italian-American to do so.)

To political analysts today, there is an important lesson to be gleaned from London's and La Guardia's first elections: they came roughly three decades after the first waves of East European Jews began arriving in New York City. By that timetable, the Asian, Latin American and West Indian immigrants who began flowing into New York in the mid-1960's are not far behind.

"By the Russian Jewish time clock, 1999 is equivalent to 1915," said

Philip Kasinitz, a Hunter College sociologist.

The Italians and Jews became politicized at different rates. Italians, like many Hispanic immigrants today, were relatively slow to naturalize, in part because many did not intend to make America their permanent home. Jews become citizens faster, in large part because they had no intention of returning to Europe. They also brought with them urban traditions of socialist politics and labor organizing that caught on with immigrants in New York City's working-class streets and sweatshops.
And while the Democratic Party was slow to recruit these Jewish and Italian immigrants, it eventually embraced them, and they it. By the 1950's, the old Democratic machine was dominated by Italians, particularly its last true boss, Carmine G. DeSapio. And Jews became important forces not only in the mainstream organization, but also in the reform clubs that produced Mayor Edward I. Koch.

In the 1960's, when strict immigration quotas were lifted, new waves of immigrants from Asia, Latin America and the West Indies began pouring into the city. And the very diversity of these immigrants has become a major hurdle not confronted by the Jews and Italians before them.

In 1933, when La Guardia was elected mayor, Italians and Jews together represented a third of New York's population. Today, Dominicans, the city's largest immigrant group, are roughly 6 percent of the population; West Indians as a group are about 8 percent. Chinese, the largest Asian group, are less than 4 percent. Unifying them will be a politician's nightmare.

The new immigrants face another challenge: the Democratic Party has been on a steady downward trend. Reform politicians have weakened the party's control over patronage, a fundamental recruiting tool. The modern welfare state has made the clubs' rudimentary social services seem redundant. Paid consultants have taken over the work of running campaigns, reducing the need for immigrant volunteers.

"We can't even fix a parking ticket," said James McManus, whose great-uncle founded the McManus Midtown Democratic Association on West 44th Street more than 90 years ago. "It's no wonder people don't come around anymore."

But for all the obstacles, the new immigrants have had their triumphs. Just this decade, the Dominicans have come to dominate politics in Washington Heights, one of the most concentrated immigrant enclaves. Dominicans virtually control the three local Democratic clubs and the local school board. They have elected one of their own, Guillermo Linares, to the City Council, and another, Adriano Espaillat, to the State Assembly.

And when Representative Charles B. Rangel retires, many local party officials predict, the area is very likely to elect the first Dominican to Congress.

And in the Bronx, the last of the city's true political machines, the county Democratic committee, which is dominated by Puerto Ricans, is trying to build citywide immigrant support behind Borough President Fernando Ferrer, who is considering running for mayor in 2001. He is a long shot, but his efforts may lay the foundations for an immigrant candidate to seek citywide office in the future. And perhaps, like La Guardia, that first successful citywide candidate will have roots in more than one immigrant group.

"This is a group of people who are hungry, who are ready for ownership of a city that has not always been kind to them," said Assemblyman Roberto Ramirez, the county chairman.

Breaking Out
Electoral Success As a West Indian
Who, many historians ask, will be the new immigrants' Meyer London?

One of the strongest candidates would seem to be a bespectacled, pixie, hard-charging mother from the island of Jamaica: City Councilwoman Una Clarke of Brooklyn, who is aggressively raising money and courting support for a potential challenge to Representative Major R. Owens, a nine-term Democrat, next year.

"They are pushing me to run," she says of her fellow West Indians, pretending she hasn't tried to stoke such talk. "Their plot is to push me so far that I cannot turn back."

In her drive for recognition, Mrs. Clarke, 64, clearly reflects the desires of many of the city's 600,000 West Indians -- particularly in Flatbush and Crown Heights -- to see their growing population translated into political power beyond the City Council or State Legislature. But by taking on Mr. Owens, who is African American, a Clarke campaign could also place her into conflict with central Brooklyn's other major voter bloc.

In the past, politicians from the West Indies -- including Representative Shirley Chisholm, an immigrant from Barbados who represented the 11th Congressional District in the 1970's -- generally viewed themselves as African-American leaders first and Caribbeans second. But for Mrs. Clarke, being from the West Indies seems to come first.

Indeed, Mrs. Clarke, who must leave the Council in 2001 under term limits, has built her career on issues related to the West Indies. In the Council, her signal achievement was to legalize the unlicensed vans that are owned mainly by West Indian immigrants. And recently, she led a delegation to Washington to lobby for trade rules that would benefit West Indian banana growers.

She also aggressively courts immigrant voters, filling her weekends with visits to West Indian festivals and interviews on local radio shows. A service in Harlem commemorating the day of Bahamian independence was typical. Midway through the event, the nation's consul general, Dr. Doswell Coakley, spotted Mrs. Clarke in the second row -- an easy task, given her bright red pillbox hat.

"Una Clarke is term-limited and moving on to other things," Dr. Coakley told the crowd as Mrs. Clarke covered her face with red-gloved hands in mock horror. "She tells me she is Caribbean first, and that we keep her in the fore of our thoughts. We shall."

Mrs. Clarke and her husband came to the United States in 1959 as students, had two children and decided to stay. Politics seemed to come naturally. She first got involved in Parent-Teacher Associations, then helped form an insurgent Democratic club that included Mr. Owens. Later she became head of a community group called the Caribbean Action Lobby.

And in 1991, after the city created a majority-West Indian Council district in central Brooklyn, she defied the county's black-dominated Democratic organization, which supported an American-born black candidate, and won the seat.

"I never saw bias until I ran in 1991," Mrs. Clarke said recently. "When I entered office, the street talk was, 'Why do these West Indians feel they have to be in politics?' "

Now, her daughter, Yvette, 34, is considering running for her Council seat. More than the mother, the daughter moves seamlessly between two worlds. "How do you like my daughter?" Mrs. Clarke asked an acquaintance recently in the lilting voice that marks her as a West Indian immigrant. "Is she an all-American girl? I'm getting there myself. It's taken a long time, but I'll get there."

Working Together
Asian Immigrants Look to Coalitions

The gathering of the North Flushing Civic Association was much like the dozens of civic association meetings held every month in Queens. A group of 60 middle-class homeowners, upset about a proposed Salvation Army church on 32nd Avenue, fired testy questions about increased traffic and ruined vistas at church officials.

But there was something different about this event: the man running it. He was John Liu, a 32-year-old immigrant from Taiwan, the association's president and one of just four Asian-Americans in the room. It is often that way for Mr. Liu, who is trying to become the first Asian-American on the City Council.

While immigrant candidates in heavily concentrated immigrant communities like Washington Heights or Flatbush can afford to focus on their fellow countrymen, Asian-Americans in Queens cannot. Not only are Asian-Americans a minority in most Queens communities; many do not vote. Even in Flushing, where Asian-Americans are nearly half the population, they represent less than 20 percent of the registered Democrats. The rest either are not citizens or have registered as independents or Republicans, making them ineligible for the Democratic primaries that usually determine elections here.

Don Nakanishi, director of the Asian-American Studies Center at the University of California at Los Angles, says that while Asian-Americans are quick to naturalize, they are slow to register to vote. The reasons he gives include a strong emphasis on work over other activities, and a fear of politics from living in authoritarian Asian societies.

Mr. Liu, an actuary, learned those lessons the hard way. In 1997, he was one of two Asian-American Democrats who challenged City Councilwoman Julia Harrison, a Democrat who had sharply criticized Asian-American business owners in Flushing on a variety of issues, including not posting signs in English. The two split the Asian-American vote, making it easier for Mrs. Harrison to win re-election with just 48 percent of the vote.

With Mrs. Harrison required to step down in 2001, Mr. Liu is working much harder to gain support among non-Asians -- not an easy task when many longtime residents bristle at the rapid growth of Flushing's Asian-American population.

So he fills his evenings and weekends with political events where he can meet and greet the borough's Democratic cognoscenti and voters. In addition to his civic association, he sits on the boards of the Queens Symphony and a handful of Democratic clubs, including one linked to the most powerful official in his Council district, Assemblyman Brian M. McLaughlin, whose support he hopes to win.

A stocky, effervescent man with a boyish face and the kind of boundless energy a good politician needs, Mr. Liu arrived in Flushing at the age of 5 when his father, a bank executive, was transferred to New York. Back then, the family was among the neighborhood's only Chinese.

"I didn't want to speak Chinese," he recalled in his unaccented English. "I wanted to be white."

29

But at the State University of New York in Binghamton, he became active in the Asian-American organization. Angry that the group was receiving far less financing than others, he and friends campaigned to pack the student assembly with Asian-Americans. They won, and the Asian Student Union got a $10,000 budget increase.

Five years ago, he and his wife, a nuclear engineer, bought an 80-year-old Colonial-style home just a few blocks from where he grew up. Sometimes he recalls the racial slurs of his childhood as he walks door to door, trying to drum up support for his incipient campaign.

"People say to me: 'I'm Italian. You are going to know what I need?' " he said. "I say: 'You need regular garbage pickup. You need the schools to be good. And you know what? That's what I want, too.' "

Joining Ranks
Hell's Kitchen Club Takes Latin Flavor

The McManus Midtown Democratic Association on West 44th Street has the musty, other-era feel of someone's well-kept attic. Outside, a red-haired man sells J.F.K. buttons. By the door hangs an oversize drawing of George Washington Plunkitt, the salty Hell's Kitchen district leader whose blunt advocacy of "honest graft" was Tammany Hall's turn-of-the-century motto. Old men sit watching television.

But on a recent evening, there was a distinctly new New York feel to the club's clientèle. A family of Mexicans sat on folding chairs inside the door, awaiting help with a housing matter. A few paces away, a club member filled out immigration forms for a Colombian woman. And in the back, a Brazilian man leafed through a sheaf of job openings at city agencies.

Carlos Manzano, the club president, looked on happily.   "I did my homework," he said, referring to the job listings he had compiled. "That's what Carmine DeSapio told me. Do your homework."

In one sense, the 33-year-old Mr. Manzano, who builds and manages World Wide Web pages for a living, is something of a political throwback, the last of a dying breed. But in another, he may be the model for something new: immigrants trying to revive the city's political clubs.

Mr. Manzano, who emigrated from Colombia in 1985, joined the club 11 years ago as a student at Queens College, simply because he wanted to learn about American-style politics. He was the club's second Hispanic member. But over the next few years, he recruited other immigrants, largely by providing basic services: citizenship classes, free legal services and assistance in navigating the city bureaucracy.

It was not quite like the old days, when clubs could put a supporter's nephew on the city payroll or get a friendly judge to go easy on a particular case. But the club's Hispanic membership grew steadily to 600, about half of its total.

This Latinization drew grumbles from some of the older Irish and Italian stalwarts. But the effort had the blessing of Mr. McManus, who had installed Mr. Manzano as president and helped elect him a district leader. To him, Mr. Manzano represents not just the future of his club, but of New York City politics.

"Nobody gave the Irish and Italians anything," Mr. McManus said, adding, "So I've been waiting for someone like Carlos to come along and do the same thing for poor and working-class Hispanics."

With that in mind, Mr. Manzano, whose ever-crisp attire and dignified bearing seem as old-fashioned as his politics, ran last February for City Council in a heavily white district that extends from West 74th Street into Greenwich Village. Derided as "the machine candidate" by his opponents, he finished second in a field of four.

Since then, he has received feelers from other Hispanic leaders about running as a pan-Hispanic Council candidate in Queens. More appealing to him is spending nights at the club. As he prepared to close down at 10:30 on a recent evening, a frail looking, elderly woman walked in and asked for a private meeting.

As they emerged from their talk a few minutes later, the woman began to toddle off, then stopped and gave Mr. Manzano a kiss on the cheek. "You will take care of that, right?" she asked. "Cause if you don't, who will?"

CHAPTER 2

SCHOOL BOARD

1996

I had been advised that one way to get involved in American politics, and New York City politics in particular, was to try to run for a seat on the local school board. I was new at the game of campaigning in American politics. But I knew I wanted to get involved in politics as a way of improving the community and since I had three daughters (Nusrat, Shaharin, and Israt) in the local public school, I had a greater incentive to see that the schools were managed properly to provide the greatest education possible for my children.

As a school board member, I would be faced with learning how to control a multi-million dollar local school district budget in Queens. I would also be responsible for determining personnel decisions about who would get hired or fired, decide as to which business proposal got chosen, and accountable for providing an effective and good education for the children. Since the school board position was an elected position by the local citizens and parents, I had to show the residents I was qualified to accomplish all these goals. In effect, the school board member position is very important because a lot of money was coming from the taxpayers.

My road to this position began when I met Arthur Rojas, a Queens lawyer and a community activist at the time. Arthur was a second-generation Hispanic whose parents had immigrated from Colombia. He was keenly aware and sensitive to the concerns of the immigrants, those I came to call the "New Americans." Arthur himself had no interest in running for any political office. In fact, it is interesting to note that years later Arthur decided to give up his career and became a Catholic priest. Although he did not want the political office for himself, he was an excellent person for any politician to have as a friend because "he knew the American political system" about how to campaign and could accomplish excellent results with his knowledge and legal expertise. Besides being a lawyer, Arthur was the president of a civic association in Queens Village. I met Arthur at one of the many civic meetings I had begun attending in Queens and we struck up a quick friendship when we learned we had mutual interests: helping immigrants, getting them registered and involved in politics, and in civic causes. As a fairly new immigrant myself, I felt I knew very well what most immigrants were experiencing in America.

Arthur began teaching me many things I needed to know about what Americans call "grassroots" politics—everything that had to be done at the local level to reach the voters. He introduced me to local political activists involved in civic groups: labor unions, teachers union, cafeteria workers union, advocacy groups, environmental groups, professional groups, political clubs, any civic group that was holding a meeting. Our goal was to connect to different people through their clubs and organizations in order to unite as a power bloc.

Arthur and I began to associate with others who wanted to run for local office. These associations with others were becoming our "coalition," as we worked at being partners for some common political objectives. The members of the coalition would bring in their friends, associates, and followers who would be willing to vote for me and the coalition.

These meetings led me to run for election as a local school board member. The decision was a natural outcome from all my exposure and connections that Arthur and I had been making, along with Chet Szarejko, a Polish-American and a leading member of the Democratic Club. His inspiration was monumental. He was like my guardian angel in my

33

activism and in my personal life. I learned much from him. I improved my political skills, and became stronger in activism through Chet's help.

In the meantime, *The New York Times* wrote a nice article entitled "Immigrants Blaze Political Trail." The article detailed my efforts and the efforts of my longtime friend, Sachi G. Dastidar, Ph.D., as we sought to win school board seats. He was running in a 15,000-student district where nearly half of the residents were white and 30 percent were Asian, while I ran in a 25,000-student district where three-fourths of the residents were black. The article also stated "the boards are open to parents who are not American citizens" (February 4, 1996). Most immigrants never knew that they did not have to be citizens in order to be on the school board at that time.

As I met many people, a few became very important in my political life: Marc Hacken, who as president of the Hilltop Coop Association in Queens, represented 1200 Jewish tenants. He could suggest to his contacts and people that they vote for me; Thelma Prescott, a former school board member since 1992, was now the principal of a nursing college on Long Island and a retired nurse. Her political strength came from the fact that she had a following after years of involvement in the Cambria Heights area of Queens; Leroy Comrie, who went on to become a New York City Councilman and Queens Borough president candidate, was at the time already a very influential person. In 1996, he was selected to be on the staff of Chief Archie Spigner, the Deputy Speaker of the New York City Council, another powerful person in city politics; and Timothy James, assistant to William Scarborough, a New York State Assemblyman. These were civic leaders and activists coming to help and they all had supporters who could vote for me. My name recognition was growing.

I gained more media exposure when a Queens newspaper *Jamaica Times* ran an article about how I wanted to be the Asian-American voice on the School Board 29 (February 15, 1996). The article explained my concerns about classroom overcrowding and the need to have immigrant parents become more involved with the school board.

34

In 1996, the New York City School Board was run a different way than it is now. The mayor had less control than he does today. Then, a candidate to the school board had to get nominated. Each local school board in the city consisted of nine members whose terms lasted for three years. The positions held enormous amount of power, considering that the board in my district affected the lives of 25,000 students.

These school board positions were coveted because they represented power over jobs, contracts, millions of dollars in budgets, and a degree of prestige in the community. Needless to say, the majority of school board members usually wanted to be re-elected and did not want newcomers to come in to start running the board differently. The position also involved interaction with the parent associations, PTA presidents, parent councils, and the local politicians.

*   *   *   *

Starting at the top, a five-member Central School Board oversaw the work of 32 school boards in New York City; a chancellor headed the Central School Board. The New York School Board represented a huge industry with a $19 billion budget, 150,000 teachers, and 1.2 million students.

The school board where I decided to run included the following: 31 schools which had about 25,000 students. Geographically, it included north and southeast Queens.

Since school board members were not paid, there was no immediate financial incentive for being a school board member, but they were given a transportation allowance (TA). The purpose of the allowance enabled the members to travel to seminars and conventions.

Interestingly, some of the school board members did not have children of their own in school. For that reason, those members might be using their position in order to gain prestige in the community and very likely set themselves up as leaders in order to run for other political offices. The school board became a steppingstone to other political ambitions.

For myself, I had several reasons for becoming a school board member: First, I had an altruistic outlook. I came to America believing that I should give back to my community and to our children. Secondly, I saw that position as a way of seeing the children improving because of our board's actions. That was very promising. Thirdly, it was a possible steppingstone for me, too, as to any possible political positions I might choose to run for later on. Fourthly, I had three daughters in public school, so I had an immediate and direct interest in education.

My "slate" consisted of three of us: Rosa Brown, a school crossing guard from the Hispanic community in Rosedale, Thelma Prescott from Cambria Heights, and me. Leroy Comrie and Timothy James each had slates of a couple of people. We were running in competition with the original school board members who had their own slate of nine, which included those on the school board up for re-election and other candidates who were their associates whom they knew would work with them in the way they wanted if elected.

I had gone out and campaigned hard. I had become better known in the civic groups, at unions, and other places, so I ended up getting the highest numbers of votes. All three of us on my slate won because I had so many votes to carry them as rollover. We had enough spillover votes that we helped other slates. For example, Timothy James got some of my votes, too.

The *Times/Ledger*, a Queens newspaper, had a picture of myself and four others being sworn in by Queens District Attorney Richard Brown as he administered the oath of office to members of School Board 29 (July 4, 1996). That picture represented a successful campaign and the beginning of our three-year term.

After the election, we formed a new coalition of two groups: Leroy Comrie's slate and my own. That way we formed a group of five people, so we became a majority on the school board. As the new majority, that meant anything we wanted we could do. Our efforts paid off to bring the Bangladesh and the South Asian community onto the map.

With our coalition holding the majority member votes, I was now voted to be the school board First Vice President. I chose not to hold the president's position on the board because the community was largely African-American and that position would be held by an African American. I preferred the First Vice President and Treasurer positions, which allowed me to stay current in the black community.

A lot of the school board incumbents were opposing me because they had different fears. They feared that I wanted to take control of the whole school board, which could affect who controls the money and who gets the jobs. Race issues were a second set of fears because the school board represented neighborhoods made up of the following ethnic groups: 84% African American, 4% white, 2% Asian, and 4% Hispanic. Those who were in a certain race or ethnic group wanted to protect and to promote what was of interest mostly to their group. Since I came from a Bangladeshi-South Asian background, those in the other races and ethnicities were unsure as to whether I would be interested in helping them. In time, they realized I had great respect for all cultures and nationalities, and I had the ability to attract the news media when we wanted to promote our issues.

Power is often hard to give up for any elected official, including the school board members who were also elected by the voters in each community. The school board had been controlled by a particular group over a period of time, so they were not about to open their arms to welcome in newcomers, especially first generation immigrants. For the most part, the South Asian and Bangladesh communities had scant or nonexistent involvement with the school boards, except for my personal involvement.

*　*　*　*

1998 Events

When in 1998 I ran to be a New York State Senator, I came into high profile again. That alarmed a lot of people because they thought I was using the school board to advance my own political interests. My political goals were not meant to "use" the school board for only personal interests. My opponents and detractors very easily forgot that I had three children in the public school and their educational needs were a primary reason I became a board member. I wanted the school to have the resources so the school, the community, and my children would do well. If the school is a good school, the prices of the houses in that area would appreciate.

I never found out at that time how many school board members even had children or grandchildren in school. Some people just looked at the school board as a place to seek power. I think four or five members on my school board did not have any children in school. There will always be those in a school board position who are there for the position's prestige and what I call "power-grabbing."

One school board member took issue with my comments about the immigrants as the "new Americans" and asked the astonishing question, "Why did they have to come here?" I had to politely overlook such snide and rude comments and put these experiences in the category of "That's all part of politics." When it comes to power, the opponents will use all kinds of negative slurs to put people down.

I won because I had what I call "a network machine." I was able to get all my people elected with me. I can't repeat it enough that everybody was surprised. Most people had discounted me as an immigrant and the people in Queens would not vote for an immigrant, although I was a United States citizen.

When I was out campaigning, people saw my energy, my enthusiasm, and knew that I was sincere about helping others.

I wanted to change the education system to accomplish the following:

- get more multi cultural programs established; create a parent training academy to improve parent, teacher, and community relations and educate everyone about reaching out to everyone about education; and increase bilingual education.

- establish computer laboratories in every school: every school classroom had a computer. That was the time that computers started coming into the schools. Some classes had more than one computer. We got some computers through the education budget and some with company sponsors.

- I helped establish a DNA-program in cooperation with Cold Spring Harbour Laboratory on Long Island and our school board. Children could learn science in new ways and in new places for field trips. Most low-performing schools had reading and writing problems. By adding this kind of science program, children learned new things, which, in turn, helped them to read better and then to write better about their experiences and what they learned. Cold Spring provided the technology and demonstrators to come to the school. Also, they trained the teachers in their facilities free of charge. There was an exchange program for the teachers and the students to go to the Cold Spring Laboratory.

- I wanted to clean up any corruption in the way contracts were granted to businesses.

North and south school districts in Queens started to respect each other. There used to be an old conflict because north Queens always had better schools than the south. Most of the board members were from south Queens. Now that I was from south Queens, I started getting the resources to the schools in south Queens. Prior to my tenure on the board, the south Queens schools were not getting the attention that they needed.

Parent involvement was important to me. I have a saying, "If parents don't get involved, children don't achieve." I strongly believe that education starts in the home. I was instrumental in helping to establish parent training courses and parent workshops with the purpose of convincing them how to behave with their children at home and how to get parents involved with their schools.

Every school has a Parent-Teacher Association that meets once or twice a month. If a parent has a problem with their children, they can talk about it. The teachers can address that problem and the children can learn how to achieve better.

I introduced that kind of program in the school. In my local area, I found that the parent-teacher meetings were not taken very seriously. There was no attention being given to immigrants and to parents in that group. No one opposed the meetings, but they were not active about implementing the program. I was serious about doing these meetings and made them a priority on my agenda. To get people and schools to cooperate, I could threaten by saying, "The results will go in the superintendent's evaluation." The superintendent would have to hold the principals and teachers accountable. I had to push.

If at any time I felt improvements were moving too slowly, I would call some of my media friends. I had a very good relationship with the media, so I would call the media to talk about the new agenda and to publicly push the community to achieve good things for their children.

The School Board Organization
The school board members used to meet once or twice a month, even more depending on important situations. In addition, the board held community and PTA meetings in the schools.

First, we had a general meeting for the public. Anybody could come and watch. We used to invite all the teachers, all the parents, all the elected officials, and all civic groups. They used to get a letter that on such a date there would be a meeting. We had a lot of parents come. They could watch, but could not give any input at that time. In a general meeting, they could comment.

We used to get letters from different teachers and organizations talking about their concerns and problems. Those concerns would give us an agenda as to what to talk about and to get done.

Secondly, we would have an executive board meeting. That gave the board time to identify our priorities. These were private meetings because there were times when we wanted to speak openly among ourselves about personnel issues and make comments that should not have to be discussed openly in public, such as appointments, firing somebody, suspensions, and sexual harassment. In addition, we dealt with any educational issue or policy.

When an important issue came up, we could have a general public hearing with about 500 to 700 people at the meeting. Some meetings were open, meaning the public could make comments. After telling the public what we were doing and what we passed, then we had a microphone and allowed the people to tell us what they wanted to say. In the end, we would take a vote in front of them.

As a board, we had our Committees, such Personnel, Budget, Special Events, and Community Relations. New ideas would be discussed in the sub-committees and then the sub-committee would bring its recommendations to the main board.

Because there were 31 schools in our district, we had a Parent Association meeting every day or evening. As board members, we had to go to those meetings to see what was happening, to learn about the concerns at the local schools, and what we could do. I had the responsibility also as the liaison for seven specific schools, but I could go into any school I wanted to. Occasionally every month, I would visit classes in different schools to see and evaluate a teacher's performance. I would visit schools without notice and report back to the board my impressions and any necessary actions to the superintendent.

Those who came to the school board meetings saw me in my public role of making decisions for the schools. However, our local citizens may not have known how much behind the scenes work has to go on to be ready for our school board meetings and some of our sacrifices. The general public probably had no idea of the sacrifices involved in being a school board member: taking off work from my job at the New York City Department of Environmental Protection and losing my compensation for the day in order to make unannounced visits to classrooms; the amount of time it took to be in meetings almost every night; time away from home and my family; and the overall expenses of eating out and the costs for using my car that were not reimbursed.

Despite the sacrifices, I appreciate the fact that I could come to America as an immigrant (a New American) and in a few years find myself on a New York City school board, making multi-million dollars decisions about the schools and the education of our youth. By the power of the vote, the local people trusted me enough to vote me to handle the school board decisions and to make a difference to improve the education. I can say this with certainty: the position requires someone who is willing to be very involved with the community and the people. On the other hand, the position automatically brought a lot of power—a school board member could change a lot of things for the community and improve the schools for future generations. To me, I had the honor of being part of New York City politics and its education decisions.

Corruption
Wherever there are multi-millions of dollars being spent and companies are bidding for part of that money, someone may come along who wants to corrupt the system. Were there those who used the school board for their own corrupt purposes? Of course. In fact, corruption by certain people came to light in the newspaper during my first tenure on the school board,.

When I first started on the board, I sensed that something was not working right, but I could not discover what it was. The "sense of something wrong" came to me in at least two ways: first, a lot of people were talking about what seemed to be illegal actions and, secondly, the resolutions I opposed were still passing in some mysterious ways.

I started complaining, "What's going on here? There's no talk, no discussion about who is bidding and how many bids we have."

In one case, the board approved spending millions of dollars to buy some computers. I did not see any information about the company, what kind of product they are going to give, and there were no other companies in the bid. This lack of information and lack of multiple bids seemed very strange and certainly questionable.

One day I went to a meeting and some board members were trying to quickly pass a resolution that this company would get the computer contract. I was surprised that we had to vote for it without further information or discussion. I opposed. Everybody else voted for the resolution.

Finally, the Inspector General's Office of New York City investigated and they found that the questionable company had bought three houses for the District Superintendent in order to get the contract. Some other people were probably involved. The fraud was reported in the newspapers and the District Superintendent went to jail.

A lot of people did not like that I was bringing this fraud to light. I asked, "How come this can happen?" Sometimes, a person is voted into office and finds out that fraud may be going on somewhere. I took a stand not to be part of the fraud. I wanted an honest and transparent education system, not one of payoffs and fraud.

After that incident, the school board tried to reinstate that District Superintendent Mrs. Celestine Miller. I said, "You can't." Because I did not want to allow any further corruption, a lot of people ended up respecting me and a lot of people hated me. Some tried to destroy me by saying, "Morshed is ruining the community." I said, "What I've done is not against any particular community. It's for the sake of the children."

* * * *

My Involvement to Bring Changes

Because of my involvement on the school board, our board worked to bring all our diverse ethnic, cultural, and communities in Queens together. It was a multi-cultural approach to education.

Also, I was petitioning for multi-lingual and bilingual education. There are a lot of children in Queens who are living in immigrant families and speaking many languages. When they come to this country and to the school, they often do not know English.

We always had the immigrants know that English is the preferred language. We arranged for a special time to learn English and specially-trained teachers for ESL (English as a Second Language). I initiated more funding so they could hire more ESL teachers and have more ESL classes for these children with special language needs.

I pushed our school board to get more money for after-school programs. Those children could be tutored at the school between 3-6 P.M., making the school something of a day care center so the parents did not have to pay for day care during that time.

I passed a resolution to improve the food: the cafeterias would serve special kinds of food for different ethnic groups in the district. There were students from Bangladesh, Pakistan, China, Korean, West Indies, and all kinds of multi-ethnic groups, so we provided food for those children. If the children don't eat, their stomachs would be empty. The special food took into consideration religious food. For example, there would be halal food for the Muslims and kosher food for the Jewish children. (Halal is like a kosher preparation and has to be prepared by a special person who knows how to prepare it according to Islamic law. Of course, ham and pork is not eaten by the Muslim children, and no meat for vegetarians.)

The school does not have to hire a special cook for the special food because the school could serve one choice of a vegetarian diet. Any

44

religion can eat vegetarian food. The food should be nutritious so the children will eat. Everyone knows the importance of food: if children get good quality food, they will be more alert in their classes.

I came to realize that I had to "buck the system" because some of the school board members did not believe in making food changes. I came along to be the catalyst to make the changes. My changes were not only about food, I was talking about improving the educational system and bringing groups together. In the end, everybody felt the changes were good and the various ethnic groups were very happy for the changes.

* * * *

1999 Events

In 1999, I was up for re-election to the school board. It was no easier running the second time. I began being opposed by every elected official because they came from certain groups, and each group had its own slate and different agenda as to what they wanted to happen at the school board meetings.

Even my friend Leroy Comrie, the one I helped to be school board president twice, could not support me because all the civic leaders of south Queens decided to get rid of me. They apparently had a nagging fear that I was going to take over the school board with my supporters. This is part of the scenario of local politics. An outsider who has never attended a school board meeting might wonder what all the fuss was about on the board.

It has to be remembered that the school board members have power over two important areas: who gets what jobs and who gets the coveted school board contracts that can run into the millions of dollars for any company. Our board had a say over about 5,000 jobs and every year we had about 500 job openings. Many South Asians began getting jobs during my tenure. We were always voting on job issues all the time.

The work that I did in my first three years was not appreciated by everyone because they saw me as a "reformer." I was the kind of person who said, "Let's change the system so that it is more open, more accountable, more pro-community, and more for the interests of the children." That was my agenda. I wanted an honest, open agenda, but others wanted things done secretly and in ways that benefited them at the expense of the schools and the children.

The subject of contracts could cause controversy because so much money was involved. There were different types of contracts—from food supply, construction, to job-related.

The school board had the power to appoint the school superintendent, the principals, supervisors, the teachers, and even the school aides. A person could get a job or lose a job through the discretion of the school board.

Every year, the school board had to find new teachers because others retired, took disability, or leave. That meant a huge employment pool that had to be filled. Obviously, those who were looking for jobs would, sometimes, want their political representative or someone on the school board to "do a favor" for them by getting them hired. Therefore, politics played a larger part in the selection process.

I become the one who opposed doing things the old way and I avoided "playing politics" in order to serve my own ends. Rather than fight with certain school board members, I realized I could stop doing things the same old way by bringing to light anything secret going on in the school board. Was I trying to be a maverick simply to be confrontational? Of course not. , because I wanted what was best for the schools, the students, and, by a ripple effect, things would become better in the communities where the students were getting a better education.

When I felt so frustrated with the school board not doing enough to improve the schools, I chose to go to the media to bring out how the school board mainly wanted to keep doing business the same old ways.

Obviously, that exposure upset some board administrators and certain politicians who did not like my doing that.

*   *   *   *

President Clinton

At that time, the school board played an important role in education, funding, and the development of the neighborhood too. Since I was part of the northern school district in Queens, that's where I would be running and where I wanted to help the district's 31 schools. Actually, my house is the last house at the border of my school board district. Nearby is the local elementary school, Abigail Adams school P.S. 131 in Jamaica, where my daughters attended.

In June, 2000, President Clinton wanted to visit two schools in the country in support of his school construction budget. He proposed bailout legislation for school construction, worth about $32.7 billion. To support his proposal, he made a visit to two schools. His staff chose a school in Harlem to show how his budget would help that well known area with its community blight and educational problems. The Department of Education offered some other choices, Jamaica, Queens.

Here is an example of how I learned about "playing politics" on the school board. Our local board wanted him to go to a school with a largely African American student population. In the school board meeting, I argued that we shouldn't have the president visit such a school because he already visited a school in Harlem and while there would come to understand the African American experience and the needs of the children. I proposed that we take the president to a neighborhood where he could see a larger variety of ethnic and cultural mixes, namely P.S. 131, a neighborhood of Asian, white, Black, and Hispanic residents. I argued that at that school he could see a real picture of the city's diversity.

There were several meetings with the school board and Clinton's people to try to resolve the issue where to visit. Ultimately, District 29

School Board Superintendent Michael A. Johnson helped to get President Clinton to P.S. 131 because he supported my idea. He said, "President Clinton should go in a neighborhood where he can see all different nationalities that connect this community together."

On June 20, 2000, President Clinton visited P.S. 131 Elementary School. The whole community was so happy to see President Clinton and, of course, I was there to greet him and to be part of the festivities. If I had not become a member and the vice president of the local school board, I am sure that the president would have gone to another school and likely one that would not have had such an ethnic mix as P.S. 131. I felt proud that I could accomplish something special for my community, our local school, and for my own children who were able to meet President Clinton. I considered the president's visit an important achievement for the local communities.

P.S. 131 ended up getting a lot of federal money. That was a reason for Clinton's visit—to show how schools could be improved with the federal money and attention. P.S. 131 became one of the best schools in the city because they got the attention from President Clinton's visit and his promised financial help. Again, I considered that my position on the school board resulted in the school and the school district in getting more money and help with programs because of my efforts. Besides money for school construction, the school received all kinds of new resources to help the students—teachers, community involvement, computers, audio visual equipment, and furniture.

One of my friends commented that I have helped the local real estate market because the neighborhood can always boast as part of its local history that a United States president came to here to visit. I was glad to have been instrumental in having President Clinton come to the school. He certainly charmed everyone and the students loved having his attention. I wonder, When will another president come here again?

As the school board's first vice president, I asked the board to make sure we got all the money we were entitled to. Sometimes, for whatever reasons, some of which may be political, a school or even a school district may not get all the money it should. With my determined efforts to oversee that things were done properly, I assured the various Queens neighborhoods in my district that they would receive financial help. As already mentioned, there were 31 schools in my district and I believe every school had been underfunded. If you believe in the future of your students and your country, you want the schools to have all the money they can get so that the children have the best education with better exposure to science, technology, and the digital world.   I saw my role on the school board as always pushing for more resources and more money. I encouraged the Bangladeshi parents to connect with the education system. I had a slogan, "No alternative other than education."

Of course, those on the school board who were accustomed to doing things the same old ways had to adjust to me. They tried for a while to push me into the corner because I was an outsider. I came from a foreign system, so they look at me in different way. They were not sure if I wanted to help them or their children. The growing internal conflict had to do with a power struggle going on. The school board members preferred covering up any hostilities they might have had for me. The former members wanted to keep their confrontations confidential and hoped that I would submit to sitting back doing nothing for three years. I had not struggled to get elected to the school board to keep doing the same old things and losing out on the money for the schools and the children. I felt I had only one alternative—to bring the power struggle to the public.

*   *   *   *

A Change in 2001

I worked on the school board for two terms. When I got an appointment as a New York City Voter Assistance Commissioner in 2001, I did not have enough time to do both jobs, so I made the decision to resign from the school board. As a recognition for all my school board work and achievements, a number of local community groups awarded me a variety of plaques as recognition of my service and of their appreciation of my efforts to make improvements.

Starting in the 1990s with Mayor Giuliani and continuing with the election of Mayor Bloomberg, the mayors were pushing the New York State legislators to give the mayor and the Central Board more control and to dismantle the local school boards.

After 9/11 and with the election of Mayor Bloomberg, times were changing. The school boards in New York City have since been dismantled by the New York State Assembly after thirty years. All power is now being handled by the Central Board and the Board of Education. For example, they are now appointing the superintendents, whereas the local school boards used to make the superintendent appointments.

The schools are now directly controlled by the mayor and the chancellor. There is an Educational Council which can voice its opinions, but they did not have any executive power. They do not represent any communities, but are simply an advisory council.

In 2001-2002, the school board had been extended until the change took effect. I looked back to having successfully campaigned and won in two school board elections. I might have likely won many more school board elections, if the school boards still existed and if I focused solely on those elections.

With the changes in the educational system and with my decision to resign in order to move into another role, I look back during my two three-year terms and believe that I achieved some excellent goals for the Queens schools and for the children. With my 2001 resignation, I went back to focusing on my role of helping the new Americans and the New York City residents to get involved with voter registration, getting out voters, and helping new candidates run for office.

Reprinted by permission from India in New York

July 4, 1997

"GOV. PATAKI HONORS COMMUNITY SCHOOL BOARD MEMBER"

BY JYOTIRMOY DATTA

When Gov. George Pataki presented the Governor's Award of Excellence to Morshed Alam at a reception in honor of Asian American Heritage Month at the ABC Building in New York on May 22, it was a recognition of the long way that Alam, a native of Bangladesh, and his community have traveled since their arrival on these shores in the 1980s.

Alam had come to America with a masters degree in soil science from the University of Dhaka in 1984. He got a job with New York City's Department of Environment, married, bought his own home in Jamaica Estates, and should have rested content with his enviable lot.

But he wanted to enhance the lives of others from his native land who had not had his advantage in education. The influx of Bangladeshis began in 1987 after the United States instituted a visa lottery; now they are perhaps the fastest growing immigrant community in the greater New York region, according to Alam.

He estimates that there are over 120,000 Bangladeshis in New York City, concentrated in Jamaica, Jackson Heights, Elmhurst and Astoria, in Queens; South Ozone Park and East Kingston in Brooklyn; Parkchester and Woodlawn in the Bronx and in downtown Manhattan.

For 300 years, the words "New York City" have spelled freedom and opportunity to people around the world; Bangladeshis are the newest group to seek to make full use of New York's opportunities.

Alam reckoned that there are approximately 150 groceries, 100 restaurants, 350 small construction companies and limousine services run by Bangladeshis in the New York area. They hold annual soccer, cricket and basketball tournaments. Bangladeshis also have half a dozen or so regular weeklies. While West Bengal's Bengali-speaking community is older, it doesn't have the thriving and self-supporting Bengali language press of the Bangladeshi community, of which "Probashi," which is in its 13th year of publication, is the oldest, and the eight-year-old "Thikana" claims to be "The Largest Bangla Newsweekly Outside Bangladesh."

The community also boosts of two temples, one church and 10 mosques. In Jamaica estates alone, they have completed work on a $1.2-million mosque and are planning to build another costing $2 million, said Alam. In his neighborhood, all new houses being put up for sale are being grabbed by Bangladeshis.

"We are here to stay, and that is why I am so involved in the future of our schools," said Alam, who last year won election to New York Community School Board 29, the first member of his community to be elected to public office in the region. Indeed, Alam won with the highest number of votes in all New York City School Districts. He is now both a member and treasurer of School Board 29.

He is deeply involved in the Queens political scene, being the community affairs director of Eastern Queens Democratic Club, and a member of the Asian American Advisory Council to Rep. Gary Ackerman.

He is also founder and president of the Bangladesh American Friendship Association, a nonprofit organization that provides language tutors, and job and medical referrals, and educates Bengali immigrants about the importance of registering and voting after becoming citizens.

The Governor's award for Alam's services to the community capped other recognitions. City of New York Comptroller Alan G. Havesi, in a commendation presented on June 18, praised Alam's "valued leadership to the community." Earlier last month, when he was honored by the Asian American Democratic Club of Queens, Bronx borough president and New

York City Democratic mayoral candidate Ruth Messinger said in a message:

"Morshed Alam's vigorous and dedicated work on Community School Board 29, his service to U.S. Rep. Gary Ackerman's Asian American Advisory Council, as well as his commitment to this club, make him one of our city's most valued public citizens."

CHAPTER 3

NEW AMERICAN DEMOCRATIC CLUB

Being on the School Board was interesting because I began experiencing how the different ethnic communities related to their schools. Before campaigning, I did not have an understanding of the African American community's concerns and interests. Because the school board at the time was 84% African-American, it was imperative that I gained a deeper and richer understanding of the African American community—their culture, politics, education, economics, social values, religion, and the perspective of their leaders.

I learned about their feelings for other communities, especially the Asian, white, and Hispanic communities. I found that their religious organizations, especially churches, played a very important role in every sphere of their life—education, politics, civics, marriage, and everywhere. Churches seemed to be the center of their social life.

As I campaigned, I came to know the African-American community's politics and their important players, especially in my area of Queens: Archie Spizner, the Deputy Speaker of New York City; Congressman Floyd Flake, a powerful black politician and a leader in the AME (African Methodist Episcopal Church); Congressman Gregory Meeks; Senator Malcolm Smith; Assemblyman William Scarbough; Councilman Leroy Comrie; Councilman James Sanders; Assemblywoman Barbara Clark. I came to know personally so many African-American leaders and they taught me how politics played a role in the African-American community. Needless to say, the African-American school board members wanted was

54

best for their schools. My experiences with these political leaders was a step forward in preparing me to do more for the Asian community.

October, 1996: Forming the New American Democratic Club

After attending the Democratic Clubs in Queens over the years, I became inspired to ask myself, How can I organize my own New American Democratic Club? My good friend, Arthur Rojas, whose parents emigrated to the U.S. from Colombia, became my friend and provided the direction I needed, including a lot of helpful advice from Chet Szarejko, a local Democratic leader.

With Arthur's help, I was introduced to and immersed into the Hispanic culture. I came to know their food, culture, religious, and civic organizations. Arthur introduced me around everywhere in Queens, especially in Jackson Heights and Corona, which had major concentrations of Hispanics in Queens.

When I was elected to the school board, a couple of Hispanics were also elected to the school board: David Glasberg, an Hispanic from District 30 and others. While campaigning, I was in contact with them and, sometimes, together we went around to the different ethnic communities: Chinese, Korean, West Indies, Trinidad, Guyanese, and Haitian. Queens has become one of the most ethnic diverse communities in the city and even the country. To have any political future, any politician in Queens must be willing to relate to all these ethnicities.

As for the school board elections, the civic organizations play a vital role in helping candidates get introduced to the community. I initially came as a stranger to the civic groups because people did not know me. Arthur, Chet, and I just kept going night after night to the different civic meetings. At those meetings, I came to understand the local issues, such as the concerns about traffic lights, street lights, street repairs, zoning, the school district, transportation, and racial issues. I have a feeling that most people do not know how interesting their community meetings can be. For me, I found that the meetings can be very vibrant as the local residents discuss and debate their issues passionately.

Before learning about all the various community groups, I also became a member of the Eastern Queens Democratic Club in 1991. By attending all their meetings over the years, I learned how a club was organized and how it conducted its business. Considering all the ethnicities, I became excited about bringing multiple ethnicities together in one place in one club. In short, I began having the vision and concept for a political club that I would call the New American Democratic Club.

I started out by inviting a few community activists to meet with me at a local restaurant in order to form our new political club. Some of my co-founders included Arthur Rojas of the Hispanic community; Pauline Chu, the president of school board 25 in Flushing for ten years and well known in the Chinese community who was also a candidate one time for the City Council; John Park in the Korean community; Julia Harrison, a Councilwoman.); and Elizabeth Aviras, from Argentina; Peter Richard; Rosa Browne and Imcha Kim, both school board members. Plus, we invited African-Americans—American blacks as well as those from the West Indies. There were about 45 of us who formed the club. It must be said that an important part of our leadership were our members who came from trade unions. Dr. Niten Charterjee was a trade union leader.

To the delight of myself and our new members, the club began getting media exposure early on in all the different newspapers.

*   *   *   *

I enjoyed politics and wanted to be something of a political leader who could make better things happen in Queens. But I had to learn some hard lessons.

56

I felt let down by two groups: (1) my fellow immigrants who still had a lot to learn about politics, especially when it came to giving money to support their candidates, and (2) the local Democratic Party itself. There may have been a third group that I just felt were jealous or ignorant who preferred complaining about community problems, but who never got involved in the civic or political groups who could bring out changes.

I think the established Democratic political leaders basically did not understand me. I came to them as a "foreigner," in that I had not been born in America. I spoke English with a slight accent. They did not know what to expect from me and whether I would fit in with their political machine, namely, conducting political business and voting the way they wanted me to do. Furthermore, I think the political leaders had a sense of confusion as to whether I could raise enough money and whether I was electable. Could a candidate outside the traditional white, African-American, or Hispanic communities get elected? They all too quickly wrote me off, thinking I could not get elected, because I had no political experience, name recognition, or connections. With that assumption, I am sure they did not want to set themselves up to be ridiculed and think that they would be wasting their campaign money by throwing it into some political black hole in support of me, the unknown candidate.

As the outsider and newcomer to the United States, I turned the tables by proving it was possible to win. I surprised everybody with my successes with the school board elections. Even as I struggled through my campaigns and wished for more help, I held onto a positive outlook that all the hardships that I experienced were important to what I needed to learn about the American political system: how to organize a community; what were the various community issues of concern; the election process; the petitioning process; campaigning; how to reach out and motivate the community people; conducting elections; and the American political system as a whole.

A lot of what I learned came from the advice of my activist friends and by doing—making the effort and making the mistakes. I don't think what I experienced was written down somewhere in a how-to manual. Running for office involves a lot that is not clear, so I had to learn the

57

process from A to Z—organizing, mailings, speaking, media contacts, attending events, campaigning, getting voters out, fundraising, issues, connections, and the unexpected things that came along unpredictably. I spent a lot of time learning the political process over the years and often had to devote as much as 60 to 80 hours a week to the political work. Four other important comments about this political work: (1) it had to be done after work at my city government job as a chemist; (2) it involved a lot of traveling around to all the communities in Queens, going street by street, door to door; (3) I traveled around the country to political events; and (3) I used a lot of my own money over the years to support my political cause, campaigns, and attending events.

I estimate I visited about 10,000 houses in Queens. When I started out, nobody knew me in any personal way, so I had the challenge of reassuring them that I should be their candidate. Eighty percent of the homes I visited I estimated were in white communities and the other twenty percent represented a mix of other races and ethnicities.

When I first announced this new Democratic Club, I held a press conference. The elected politicians came because everybody was curious to see what kind of new group this was all about and the politicians were especially interested in finding out how this group could help them in their campaigns. We were new even as the name said and the politicians didn't know who we were. As we presented our agenda, the media and the politicians were surprised to see our zeal, our understanding of the system, and the active participation of new groups in politics.

Still, our club had the big job of teaching our own immigrant communities that they could and should get involved with the civic causes and the political system. We had to do a lot of teaching—about the system, the necessity about their involvement, overcoming their fears about political involvement, and how to be activists. So much of the work came down to education- education-education of the people. We did voter registration. We went around talking about taking their citizenship seriously, their responsibilities as citizens, their political rights, the importance of voting, teaching them how to choose a candidate, and who to support based on the issues. There are some issues that are very important, such as housing. Housing is so important to everybody no matter one's race, color, or ethnicity. Public education is another important issue, including how can children and adult immigrants get to better education.

*   *   *   *

In 1992, I gained more political participation and experience by being part of President Clinton's New York City Fundraising Committee as a fundraiser and member of the Democratic National Committee (DNC) Asian-American group.

In 1994, our club helped with fundraising for Governor Mario Cuomo. We did the fundraising for David Dinkins, the New York City mayor. We helped all the elected officials from Queens: Congressman Gary L. Ackerman, Congressman Anthony Weiner, Congressman Gregory Meeks, and Congressman Joseph Crowley. We raised money for Councilmen, Assemblymen, and whoever ran for state senate. As a club, we endorsed them and we helped them by getting out the votes, campaigning, and inspired people to be volunteers.

Many people coming from Third World countries are not used to this political process or the idea of volunteering. They don't understand about the fundraising process, volunteerism, and speaking out about the issues— housing, education, health, abortion, anti-abortion, choice, pro-choice, jobs, environment, racism, and any issue that affects our lives.

In 1998, I decided to run to be a state senator.

In 2000, our New American Democratic Club claimed a big achievement when we won an election: John Liu, a Chinese American, became a City Councilman from Flushing, Lee Roy Comnie,a Jamaican immigrant, won from South Jamaica, and Hiram Monserrate won from Jackson Heights. Because of club's activism and our inspiration to the immigrant community, a lot immigrants came out and voted for these candidates and they won. I am proud to say that my endeavors and work paid off with the election of my friends.

Immigrants from some countries cannot go back to their home countries and run for political office. But the complete opposite is true in this country. Immigrants can come here and run for political office. In this country, everything seems possible, except they cannot be the president or vice president because the Constitution prohibits them holding those offices. In one interesting case, the governor of Louisiana came from India. He was a Congressman for two years and then a governor. Americans can proudly say, "That is only possible in this country."

*   *   *   *

My Political Connections Beyond the Club

Chet Szarejko came to the U.S. from Poland at age two. Besides becoming a high school teacher, he became a Democratic Party District Leader, a Democratic Party State Committeeman, and a famous activist in New York City. Chet became my inspiration and a mentor as he helped me to understand the local Democratic Party machine.

Chet never had the desire to run for an elected office, but I had a strong desire to get involved in politics. By making becoming a candidate, I became a local political celebrity, not just to my neighborhood, but in many other Queens communities and New York City.

My personal contacts began to include the well known people in New York City, such as George Soros, the Greek billionaire, Peter Vallone, the former New York City Council president, and his son Peter Vallone, Jr., who has also served as a New York City councilman, and the City Controller, Bill Thompson.

Union Affiliations

I have been a union activist and a professional environmentalist. I was honored to have been elected as the president of a union that represents 800 chemists, engineers, and scientists. In addition, I served as a delegate to the Local 375 union in New York City. By involving myself in the unions, I attended all the union meetings and learned the role of unions in politics and the issues of our lives, as well as learning how they negotiate their policies for their members.

The Honor of Attending the National Democratic Conventions

In 1992, I attended the Democratic National Convention for the first time. I was part of the New York State delegation and each convention has had about 350 delegates representing New York State.

In 2000, I was a delegate to the Democratic National Convention in Los Angeles and in that delegate position I became the first elected delegate from the Bangladesh community in a Democratic National convention to support Al Gore as president. My wife and daughter accompanied me to Los Angeles during the 8-day convention.

In 2004, I had the honor once again of attending the Democratic National Convention, which at the time was held in Boston. It lasted about five days with lots of seminars and meetings going on. The conventions are for learning, networking, and meeting all the powerful people, including of course senators, Congress representatives, governors, mayors, and power players. They give seminars about how to organize the voters, how to talk to rally the people, and how to deal with the media and information.

The local party leaders choose who will be their delegate by getting to know their local members and evaluate the potential of the person to make a good delegate. They consider his name recognition. They pick someone based on who has the most potential to influence his local voters; who can make party decisions; who understands the issues and the system; and who is in the community for a long time working for the party. The goal of picking delegates is to choose those who can help to elect the president.

Not only the president, but the person can help to direct the issues and who can help to get the community to get out on election day for the ticket.

Every day at the conventions so many different things are happening. A delegate gives his or her commitment and consent. The delegates voice what they see in their communities and what are the problems.

For example, immigration has become an important issue. Delegates have to discuss how they want the National Democratic Party to deal with immigration issues and they discuss what kind of immigration policy the party should take that will help their communities. I represent the new American community, so I have to discuss these issues for the national level. That is a sample of the part I played in the Democratic Party Convention.

Two Ways of Becoming a Delegate

At the primary voting, the voters simply cast votes for who would be a party delegate. Those persons with the most votes gets to go. Each congressional district elects two men, two women, and two alternative delegates.

A second option used by the New York State Democratic Committee is to have a convention in Albany. During the state convention, somebody would submit my name. I have been fortunate to have been elected at those conventions to be a delegate at the national conventions, which I have attended regularly. Those names which are submitted represent those of us who have done a lot of work at the local level and have come to have a high-level of understanding of the political system of this country. All the conventions have taught me more about the American political system about how someone gets nominated and how somebody gets elected.

Involved With Many Types of Activists

I was appointed the Chairman of the New American Committee of Queens County Democratic Party. The late Congressman Tom Menton, the chairman of the Democratic Party, made that appointment. Tom was of Irish heritage and an excellent gentleman. He realized after my 1998 election to the school board that I had a lot of power. When I came close to winning the state senate position, he gave me a lot of respect.

I see myself as an activist in many roles—union activist, environmental activist, and civic activist. As a civic activist, I like being involved in the various local issues, such as beautification of the community to traffic congestion. The New American Democratic Club is also organized as a civic club, so we discuss all issues, not just politics.

People have their opinions about illegal aliens. Our club has chosen to fight for immigrant voting rights in New York City. The legal immigrants should have voting rights because they are paying taxes. They have everything, except they don't have citizenship. They should know about where their tax money is going and they should participate in the local elections. They should elect someone who is helping their needs and their community.

New York City is made up of a 65% immigrant background. Whether legal or illegal, those living and working in New York City and paying their taxes should get their driver's license. Our club wrote a letter and showed organized support for the elected officials stating our position and what our club says carries some weight because we can rally the voters to vote for candidates who support our concerns. Of course, we discuss any issue that we see as important, not just immigration issues.

After the club members talk about an issue and come to some conclusion, we send a letter to the elected officials. To get attention to an issue, we take to the streets to hold demonstrations. Sometimes, our message works and, sometimes, it doesn't work. But we don't hold back to express our concerns.

Our club has the main purpose of asking people to be part of this country and their participation shows their love for this country. We try to remind people: Don't look at this country as a place just to make money. Look at your own life and look at the life of your community. If we are not part of helping the community, we are not really doing anything.

For example, people do not understand why a Title I or a Title II federal grant can be important to the schools. Our club tries to explain why we need more federal money. With the federal money, our students can do better. If the students are doing better, it shows that the local people are involved and their children are achieving. A good local educational system affects house buying. Parents do not want to buy a house in a bad school district. Therefore, we try to educate the people that they have a stake in their house values when they participate. If they don't participate, they should not complain about the schools, their children's education, and their house values. If they don't vote, they should not complain. That is the message I keep giving out again and again.

With my years of political, civic, and union activist experiences and skills, I am now working as a consultant to other politicians to help them get elected, along with working with others who want me to lobby at the city, state, and federal levels.

New York Daily News, L. P. used with permission

August 3, 1997

BOROUGH'S NEW DEMOCRATS

BY PAUL H.B. SHIN

In the steamy basement of an Indian restaurant in Queens Village, an ambitious group of Democrats last week recreated a modern-day version of the proverbial smoke-filled back room of Tammany Hall.

This being Queens in 1997, however, the cramped room was filled not with smoke, but with the aroma of exotic curries drifting down from the bustling kitchen, and with two dozen people hailing from the four corners of the globe.

This was the humble setting for the debut of the New Americans Democratic Club—a group formed to strengthen political ties among the city's dizzying array of ethnic communities and to bring more immigrants into mainstream civic life.

Humble beginnings aside, the group has set its sights on nothing less than changing the political landscape of Queens.

The club is the brainchild of Morshed Alam, a Bangladeshi immigrant who has made a name for himself in Queens as a community activist.

He founded the Asian American Democratic Club in 1994. "But I still felt it was too narrow," said Alam, who received a Governor's Award of Excellence on May 22 for his community service.

Though a third of New Yorkers are foreign-born, none of the individual ethnicities enjoys a commanding majority as a voting block, said Alam.

Among Hispanics, for example, the Dominicans formed the largest immigrant group to the Big Apple from 1990 to 1994, with 110,140 newcomers, according to the U.S. Immigration and Naturalization Service.

But the growth of new immigrant groups has yet to be reflected in the ranks of the city's elected officials.

"It's high time we start to participate in the mainstream of politics, being a part of mainstream politics instead of being apart from mainstream politics," said Arthur Rojas, a second-generation Colombian-American and first vice president of the new club.

"We're part of the American experience. We're reviving it with out vital energy, and you can see that all over this borough—this most diverse of counties in the United States."

Rojas, an attorney, is also well known as an activist in the Hispanic community. He is a four-term member of Community Board 13 and board member of the Queens Hispanic Coalition.

By awakening politically dormant communities, Alam and Rojas are also credited with helping Rosa Browne become the first Colombian-American elected to a school board in Queens, Board 29.

"We showed American politics how it could be, how it should be," Rojas said. "Americans of different ethnicities, of different religions and even different philosophies coming together for the common good."

Politics makes strange bedfellows.

Nowhere is this truer than in New York City, where a thousand voices clamor to push their agendas onto center stage.

But group leaders say that by focusing this discordant energy, they hope to affect the city's political agenda, especially in issues of interest to immigrants.

The group's first order of business, Alam said, is to expand its membership, which currently numbers about 50. Next in line are voter registration drives and citizenship education programs, he said.

"The future of the county really lies with the large, large number of people who are first-generation Americans," said Councilman Sheldon Leffler (D-Hollis), one of a number of elected officials who attended the club's inaugural meeting on Tuesday.

Leffler, a long-time ally of Manhattan Borough President Ruth Messinger, came to the meeting bearing a message from the mayoral hopeful encouraging the people she called "Democratic Party stalwarts" to keep up the work of expanding the party's base.

"We need more of these targeted efforts to engage people to join our party," Messinger wrote in her letter.

But leaders of the New Americans Democratic Club also made it clear they were willing to part ways with the party line if necessary.

For example, in the upcoming 20th Council District race, centered in Flushing, the group is backing Pauline Chu instead of long-time incumbent Julia Harrison, who has represented the district since 1986. Harrison has received the endorsement of the Queens Democratic machine.

But club leaders are quick to emphasize that its choices will not be made purely along ethnic lines.

"We're here not to be a divisive force, but to be a cohesive force," said Nithiananda Chatterje, an Indian immigrant and a labor leader from Staten Island. "In order to stand up, we have to stand together."

July 24, 1997

DEMOCRATIC CLUB FORMED TO TAP VOTING POWER OF CITY IMMIGRANTS

BY MARTIN MBUGUA

The first Asian member of Community School Board 29, Morshed Alam, recently formed the New Americans Democratic Club (NADC), Inc. in an effort to involve immigrants in the political process.

The new club which will be officially launched at a press conference in Queens Village on Tuesday, July 29th, aims to "integrate immigrants into American society and empower them in American politics as Democrats."

Alam, the club's president, said he started thinking about forming the club in 1990, after he started a bipartisan political group. In 1992, Alam abandoned the idea of courting both Democrats and Republicans and formed the Asian-American Democratic Club.

"But I felt that it was not enough and I wanted to do something for all immigrants," he said. "In the last seven years I was trying to form a bipartisan group but it was not working out."

Alam said the new club is geared towards utilizing the potential in the growing numbers of new Americans in Queens.

"We believe that the Democratic Party can provide a political home for them, especially given the intolerance and animus towards immigrants from other political forces," he added.

"The Republican Party has not been very helpful to immigrants. We have to help the Democratic Party but we also have to change attitudes within the (Democratic) party because they think immigrants are automatic Democrats," he said.

Alam said immigrants are often taken for granted even though they make up 40 percent of the city's population. Queens, he added, "is a haven for immigrants and the next generation of New Yorkers will be immigrants."

The school board member pointed out that 42 percent of students in School District 26 are immigrants and so are 90 percent of the students at P.S. 95 in School District 29.

Alam said it is important to make sure that tomorrow's voters are given proper direction and directed away from the Republican Party.

"Immigrants form a very strong voting block and they need to use that power so that they can get a fair piece of the cake," Alam said.

"When I ran for office as a school board member, I received the largest number of votes even though most of the voters are Haitians, West Indians and Indians," he said. "They are not racist and they are very well informed about their interests."

The new club has 40 members, most of whom are community activists. The club is expecting the numbers to swell as each of the members spread the word about it.

"The NADC will not operate within a given district or territory," Alam said. "It's focus is on a group of people who live all over New York City—immigrants or new Americans. Nevertheless, the club's primary area of activity will be Queens County for the time being."

Alam explained that the club will be involved in voter registration activities as well as encouraging voters to cast their ballots during elections.

Other club officials include Arthur Rojas, Pauline Chu, Nithiananda Chatterjie, Sachi Dastidar, Awilda Velez-Chowdhury, Mei Sim Ngai and Rosa Browne.

Reprinted by permission from India in New York

August 1, 1997

NEW AMERICANS DEMOCRATIC CLUB SWINGS INTO ACTION IN CITY

BY MATTHEW STROZIER

You might say that the recently formed New Americans Democratic Club arrived just in time. The club, which held its first press conference Tuesday night in Hollis, Queens, will attempt to build political power fro immigrants amid a contentious national and local debate about whether government should give welfare to legal immigrants and how illegal immigrants can be stopped.

"In this climate of intolerance and nativism, it is important for immigrants to get involved more than ever," said Arthur Rojas, the club's first vice president. "We believe that the Democratic Party can provide a political home for them."

The club also steps into a mayoral campaign and a number of local city council races that will test the political power of recent immigrant communities, including a City Council race in Flushing in which three Asian candidates are running to unseat council member Julia Harrison.

The club's president, Morshed Alam, said the club will be concentrating on voter registration for this election cycle, and will hold off endorsing candidates in most races, except for the city council race in

Flushing. In that race the club plans to endorse its second vice president, Democratic candidate Pauline Chu.

Alam, who is an immigrant from Bangladesh and a school board member from Queens, said he started the club because he felt that Asian Americans, to have political power, need to be part of a "bigger coalition."

At the more established political clubs, Alam said Asians and other immigrants feel alienated by "cultural barriers."

"If a club is headed by a Bangladeshi or a new immigrant—as Morshed Alam is—you entice more people to join," said Chet Szarejko, the district leader for the Eastern Queens Democratic Club, which has 500 members. "We like to have more Democrats in Queens County."

Alam said he is not worried that the cultural and religious differences that exist between many of the club's members will ultimately tear the group apart.

If there are hundreds of groups wanting to do something, then I want to help them," Alam said.

The club has about 40 members, most of whom, Rojas said, are either Asian or Hispanic. Rojas said he expects the club will reach out to immigrants from European and African countries to make the club more inclusive.

Council member Sheldon Leffler, who attended the press conference and has recognized Alam for his community work, said the club has more to do before it can be considered powerful.

"The fact that somebody is originally from China or from India does not mean that they are going to have more in common with somebody who's been in New York City for three generations," he said. "It's one thing to form a club. It's another to get elected and have real impact."

But Leffler said its "the beginning of a process" in Queens of a new generation of immigrants coming into political power.

"It's not an immediate changing of the guard," he said. "I think that's premature."

Like Leffler, various politicians showed up to welcome the club to the Democratic Party. Council member Archie Spigner and Mark Weprin were on hand and Assemblyman Brian McClaughlin sent a representative.

Leffler read a letter from Ruth Messinger, who was holding a fundraiser in Manhattan for her mayoral campaign.

The club has a large pool of potential members from which to recruit. According to the city's Department of Planning, 33 percent of the city's population is foreign-born.

CHAPTER 4

STATE SENATOR CANDIDATE

While a high school student and later as a college student in Bangladesh, I had participated as an activist in two major political changes in my country: helping those fighting to secure the independence of Bangladesh from Pakistan and, after that accomplishment, helping to organize rallies and demonstrations to replace the subsequent military regime with a democratic government. Being an activist is in my blood.

Hundreds of thousands of people died fighting for the independence of Bangladesh. Patrick Henry made his famous statement for American independence when he shouted, "Give me liberty or give me death!" Those words still express the sentiment in millions of people's hearts today when they fight for the independence of their country.

*　*　*　*

When I came to the United States, I continued my strong interest in politics, but this time I had a new zeal to use my American freedom to open up opportunities in politics. Besides, my desire to be an American politician, I also saw politics as a way of helping people and communities.

I came to learn that in American democracy someone does not just happen to get elected because their name is on the ballot. The fact is a lot goes on as to whose name gets on the ballot. I often tell people there are

73

groups of people controlling the elections. That startles some people, but it's not meant to be a cynical statement. The truth is that American politics is built around "interest groups." Those groups who are well organized and connected with the media get their message heard. If the candidate supports certain groups, that candidate gets the votes of those interest groups. From local to national politics, everything has some sort of connection to interest groups.

In the Democratic club, I continued learning several things:

- the party's structure—who held the power to make decisions
- being an activist—voter registration and political demonstrations
- the process of democracy—the laws involving candidates and elections
- the power players in the city and state—meeting them personally; learning about their character; the issues they supported; and how to deal with them.

In the party's hierarchy, the Queens Democratic Club is controlled by certain established individuals who have held power for many years. In the end, only a small group makes the decisions.

I had a simple desire of wanting to become someone in the political system and to make a difference by helping others. These were the same reasons I campaigned for a seat on the school board. In order to run for any office, I had to understand the following:

- the electoral system
- how to campaign
- power politics

By 1992, I had also founded a nonprofit organization—the American Bangladesh Friendship Association that provided different services for new immigrants:

immigration/advocacy

74

> citizenship/empowerment
> voter registration/voter education/get out the vote
> job references
> health care references
> referrals to meet any requested need

As an immigrant, I had experienced some problems adjusting to my new life in America, so I could empathize what most immigrants were going through. Some immigrants have a lot of problems for whatever reasons, so they used to call the association. Most of the time I would be the one helping.

Although I put in a lot of hours helping the immigrants and contacting other groups on their behalf, my work at my association enabled me to build a network of contacts and got me thinking. I saw both the immigrants and the other activist groups as a neglected political base ignored by the established politicians. I thought, These people will vote for me, especially when they have seen firsthand how hard I have been working on their behalf.

In July, 1997, *Newsday* helped to give me some media exposure when the paper reported about my efforts to form a multinational political club. The paper reported that "in 1995, 33 percent of the city's population was foreign-born." Our club would be going up against the well established old ethnic groups—the Irish, the Jews, and the Italians. However, my idea of forming the New American Democratic Club was lauded as a new idea and one worth watching to see what will happen.

*   *   *   *

The time came when the incumbent New York State Senator Frank Padavan would be running for re-election. He had been a state senator for about twenty-five years and had been a rather popular city politician, even though he was a Republican in a city that prides itself in voting mostly Democratic. As a Democrat, I thought it would be interesting if I could challenge him in the election. I was confident by now that I could get some support from the immigrant community on whom I counted as my base of voters. In checking Frank Padavan's background, I was shocked to find out that he had no interest in immigrants and that he considered immigrants to be a financial burden on the city. Without hearing more, I considered him right away as a major political rival that had to be defeated.

The New York Times wrote an editorial about my struggle to get on the ballot and the infighting to get people off the ballot. The editorial states, "A Democratic novice Congressional candidate named Dick Collins temporarily managed to knock the incumbent Republican, Sue Kelly, off the ballot for failing to put numbers on her pages of signatures" (August 16, 1998). The political waters can be very treacherous and can be disastrous if a candidate does not do everything correctly, which means knowing how to stay on the ballot once there.

Civic groups are normally non-partisan. As the president of the Queens Village Civic Association, my friend Arthur Rojas had the reputation of being a very controversial, outspoken, spirited activist. If an issue bothered him, he would confront anybody about it. He didn't care. His confrontational style resulted in a lot of people liking him and a lot of people hating him. I further respected Arthur because he put education as his number one issue. Having three daughters in school, I had a determination to see that they got an excellent education, so we stood together on that issue. On social issues, I found Arthur to be very conservative, whereas, I like to be in the middle ground. I don't see myself as a conservative or a liberal.

I approached Arthur and said, "I'm thinking of running for some office."

"What office do you want to run for?"

My answer would be based on the fact that I had established what I considered an excellent reputation for myself in the Queens community and throughout New York City: I had my own political club (New American Democratic Club); I had my Bangladesh nonprofit association; I had been a active member of the Eastern Democratic Club; and I had been elected to the school board, had been a union activist, and an environmentalist.

Furthermore, my years on the school board had helped me gather momentum for my other political ambitions. The school board position represented an important community leadership position because school board members made decisions that would affect important issues and many groups, including a multi-million dollar budget, contracts, 35,000 students, and 6,000 employees. I took my role on the school board seriously and had meetings with other school board members, community board members, and elected officials. Again, through the process of participation, everybody in the school district and the city had either met me or heard of my name.

When Arthur asked me what political position I wanted to run for, I said, "I don't have any money, but I want to run for the State Senate. I want you to be my campaign manager." He readily agreed.

As my first step to get started, I arranged a meeting with the Democratic Party. I wanted to run against a Republican incumbent who had a good reputation in state politics. However, I wanted to show this State Senator that he was wrong taking his very anti-immigrant stand and making immigrants out to be the enemies of New York State. He had written two books against immigrants. Also, he had sued the federal government for $5 billion to compensate New York State. He said that policies giving services to the illegal immigrant community was causing the state to lose money. As an immigrant myself, I could not let him get away putting blame on the immigrants for New York State's and the City's financial problems. I felt the passion to fight what I considered to be a legitimate cause.

Along with immigrant advocacy groups, I participated in demonstrations and marches on behalf of the immigrants and aliens. In a meeting in 1994, all the immigrant community groups decided to have someone run against Padavan and give out our message on behalf of the immigrants and the poor people.

I knew that being a New York State Senator did not represent an easy job. I think the worse part of the position is that it only lasts two years. That means every two years you have to organize people and run campaigns again. Feeling enthusiastic about my cause, I calculated that in my political district in Queens I would be facing the challenge of trying to reach a population of 350,000 and about 175,000 registered voters.

In order to run a successful campaign, I wanted to ask for the help of the leaders of the Queens County Democratic Party, specifically the chairman and the executive director. I arranged a meeting and took Marc Hagan, another community activist, with me to our official meeting where I laid out my plans. I had already formed a campaign committee, a rainbow coalition of people from all backgrounds, including Marc Hagan, a Jewish-American, Chet Szarejko, a Polish-American, and some activists from the Black and Hispanic communities.

Before the meeting with the Queens Democratic Party leaders, I had also contacted all the immigrant groups and told them, "We have a decision for 1994. We need to put up a good candidate to run for office. Do you have any candidate? Bring him or her in and I'll support them." When they told me they had no one in mind, I came back to them and said, "I'm going to run. Let me go for it." The different groups said they could help me.

In a very short time, I realized the other community groups could not follow through on their pledge to help me. In fact, no advocacy group helped me. I went back to them and asked, "Why aren't you willing to help me to run against the state senator?" Their reply came down to one word— fear. As much as they wanted to help me, they said, "All the funding will be stopped. We're getting some funding from the state, but the state senator, if he wins, could stop the state money that we count on." They were scared to death that there would be political retaliation.

At the meeting with the Democratic Party leaders, they told me, "You are not ready. The incumbent has been in office for twenty-five years. Why are you running? You will only get 10% of the votes because you are not known to the voters."

After working for the party and winning my school board elections, I felt I deserved to try. They would not budge from their position. I told them, "I will prove your prediction to be wrong. You will find it will be a different story." My secret ace I held had to do with my base of immigrant voters. I had not spent all the years working for the Democratic Party to be told by a couple of party leaders that I was still not qualified to participate in the American political system. I felt angry, upset, and frustrated.

Although I had my own setback with the political leaders, I continued meeting with the new immigrants. In my talks with them, I continued encouraging them to participate as much as possible in politics. I kept pushing them to learn the American style of politics, that is, to fully understanding the system, knowing how to dress, how to deal with each audience, and how to talk intelligently. From meeting people, the media, and attending events, everything has its appropriate codes of conduct, and, of course, rules of conduct exist in every country.

Arthur and my good friends were always a big help educating me about politics and the system. I also had a consultant group giving me some advice about my campaign plans. I did not have to hire them because we had become friends over the years. Sometimes, I got help from Bill Lynch, the campaign manager for David Dinkins, the New York City mayoral candidate at the time.

I reached out to others who might help me for free. Kevin Quang and Jack Schinder, Assistant Campaign Managers for Mario Cuomo, helped me. They were giving me solutions free of cost. Elizabeth Avers, a commissioner for David Dinkins, also helped. I had lots of people in my campaign organization and they were all giving me their help.

In addition to running, I worked a full-time job. After work, I would meet Arthur and we would take turns driving around to 6 to 10 meetings every evening which he had set up. I would speak for five to ten minutes and then we would be off to the next meeting. The whole campaign was a two-man show.

Arthur helped to do all the jobs a campaign manager needed to do: write my speeches, get our information printed, and organize the campaign financing. I used to collect the money from my own community of friends that I knew and they gave me about $35,000. Of course, Arthur had to spend more than that to run the campaign.

We were getting a lot of help from the media. The media gave me an enormous amount of exposure. In the whole city, I seemed to be a new person running for office, so I got more attention. I attracted media attention because it seemed that the Democrats were afraid to oppose the incumbent, Padavan, but I was looking like some Lone Ranger running unafraid to oppose him.

On March 21, 1998, I was prepared and set a date to declare my candidacy in front of P.S. 131 in Jamaica. One of my campaign managers resigned after being influenced to do so by the Democratic Party power brokers. I was forced to cancel my declaration, which resulted in the news media giving negative coverage. Apparently someone told them that I was going to drop out of my campaign.

The Democratic Party made an attempt to get a candidate, but they failed because nobody wanted to run. Still, the local Democratic groups did not support me. They didn't entertain me to give me a chance to talk. They didn't call me as a speaker. They didn't endorse me. They didn't help me. They did nothing and kept discouraging me from trying to run.

Meanwhile, I built my own machine throughout the district. I called on and got help from a wide variety of groups: the Sierra Club helped me on election day by providing 36 volunteers who came from Manhattan; I got volunteers from Local 375, my own union; people from a lot of ethnic communities—my Bangladesh, Hispanic, Black, Guyanese, Philippine, and Southeast Asian. They all sent me volunteers. I built my own campaign groups. The handled the job of distributing posters and fliers. I established a campaign committee called "Morshed Alam for New York State Senate."

Getting on the ballot took a lot of work because it requires asking people to sign a petition that they might be willing to vote for me. Arthur, Marc, and I did the hard work for the ballot. We hired a group of people to collect petitions for us and the signatures to be on the ballot. We collected about 1600 signatures. To compound the difficult work of getting accurate signatures, many immigrants are illegal and not registered voters.

As an attorney and an activist, Arthur Rojas knew about the intricacies of preparing the proper petitions. Together, we did the petitions. Some people from an attorney's office helped to bind the petitions. The day we submitted the petitions to the Board of Elections we were praying that no one would protest our names. If we had a problem, such as the registration of false names, I would be thrown off the ballot. We did not know how many signatures were good and, to be on the ballot, we had to produce at least 200 good signatures. The rules said that there should be at least 4800 signatures submitted in case the Board or one's opponent challenges the signatures and they are thrown out. We only had 1600 signatures, which did not give us a lot of room in case any signatures were thrown out. In the end, the Board of Elections approved my being on the ballot.

After the Board of Election approved my being on the ballot, we started campaigning. Frank Padavan had never heard of me in state politics and probably someone told him that I was a simple immigrant with no experience, so I could only assume that Padavan and his people were having a good laugh over me. I was the new guy on the block and nobody had any idea what I could do in a state election. Arthur Nitzburg, an editor of the *Queens Courier* wrote an editorial predicting that I would not even get ten percent of the vote. Although I had been on the School Board for one term, most comments were pessimistic about my opportunities to win.

I do have to take a moment to recognize the work of my wife in helping me with my political efforts. She went out on the streets and door-to-door to canvas for signatures and collected 600 signatures alone. She was used to collecting signatures because she had also done it for the school board race and knew how to register Democrats, which was a criterion. In the senate race, she worked days and nights collecting signatures, giving out literature, talking to people, and getting people to vote.

One evening I came home to find a WNBC Channel 4 TV crew outside my home who wanted to interview me with the intention of having me talk against the Democratic Party. It seemed that some in the media did not think it was right that my Democratic Party did not support me. I, too, felt a great disappointment with my party. However, I chose to take a neutral position and not sound overly critical of the party.

Newsday called U.S. Senator Patrick Moynihan's endorsement of me as "a rare endorsement in a local political endorsement." The article quotes Moynihan as saying, "I have chosen to make an exception in this case because of your [Alam] compelling record of proven leadership in the labor union movement, your local community school board and the Democratic party" (October 23, 1998).

Even though my party leaders did not endorse me or provide financial support, I still had well known politicians and groups endorsing me: Mark Green, a mayoral front runner; U.S. Senator Chuck Schumer; Comptroller Alan Hevesi; U. S. Senator Daniel Moynihan; Sierra Club; Local 375; Mark Weprin; David Weprin; State Assemblyman William Scarborough; and Congressman Gary Ackerman. They endorsed me because they knew my service to the community.

Whether I won or not, I had become overnight a political celebrity in the city. I Everybody gave me attention. After the election, people were coming to me to talk about how I did it. The civic groups, trade unions, political clubs started to call me to have me to speak about my experience. As of now today, anybody who is running in the city comes for my endorsement, for my help, and for my expertise.

Newsday published an article about my work at trying to get the new Americans to vote and how well I had run a campaign. Councilman Sheldon Leffler (D-Hollis) is quoted in the article as saying, "I think one day we will look back at this [campaign results] 15 years from now and people will say Alam was a trailblazer" (November 13, 1998).

*   *   *   *

The results of the election showed some interesting statistics. The incumbent Padavan lost in the southern part of the district where I had my main support base. In the northern part of the district, I lost because of a lack of money to campaign. The overall results showed I got 42% of the vote! That was an enormous accomplishment for someone without the party's support and someone who happened to be an immigrant. I've been told no one has beat my 42% of the vote based on the same circumstances. It is interesting that the district where I ran had 65% registered Democrats and 35% Republicans.

Channel 4 WNBC News investigated my situation and concluded that racism did play into the Democratic Party decisions. Since the party did not have any strong candidate for the state senate race, they should have supported me instead of ignoring me. If I could have had the support of the party's machine to get out the vote and another $50,000, I probably could have won easily. If I as an unknown managed to get 42% of the vote doing everything on my own, imagine what could have happened with the Democratic Party's help.

Padavan, as a responsible and shrewd politician, suddenly woke up to the political reality around him. The immigrant had almost gathered enough votes to defeat him. My Republican opponent Padavan ultimately changed his views about immigrants for two reasons: (1) he finally understood my message about the importance of the immigrants and (2) his son married an Indian woman. He now has two grandchildren. Ironically, he cannot deprecate the immigrant community without hurting his own grandchildren. Over time, I had worked to educate him about the immigrant community. He is very tolerant towards the immigrant community now.

The last Democrat who ran against Frank Padavan spent about $480,000 and got 36% of the vote. I wondered there for a while if the party leaders would finally ask me to run again, but they never did ask. The local Democratic leaders said they were going to do something for me, but they never did. The problem, as I see it, is that they still want to hold on to their own power. They don't want to bring in someone who wants to something for the people.

As for our successes at the New American Democratic Club, I can say that we helped three candidates that we endorsed get elected as city council members.

When I ran for the state senate, the immigrant community began to understand the importance of voter registration and going to the polls. I believe I have helped initiate other immigrants to run for office.

In Queens, immigrants play an important part in every election not only because the elections are very close now, but the immigrants make up such a large percentage of the Queens population. The Democratic Party is starting to understand the importance of uniting the immigrants. Again, I've learned over the years about motivating the immigrant community to vote and have taught them why we endorse certain candidates.

CHAPTER 5

COMMISSIONER OF VOTER ASSISTANCE OF NEW YORK CITY

In 2001, I had the honor of the Queens County City Council delegation, which is made up of 14 councilmen (13 are Democrat), propose my name to be the Commissioner of Voter Assistance of New York City.

The first step required the submission of various names to be a Commissioner of Voter Assistance. Those names are sent to the Department of Investigation. It took several months for my background check: voter registration, driver's license, tax returns, work, community reputation, and mortgage. Once they were satisfied, they sent the information to the City Council Election Subcommittee. That committee held hearings at which time the city council members came and endorsed me. The Election Subcommittee held its own election and passed a resolution to choose me. They then submitted my name to the full council. They voted 49 to 0 in my favor. My appointment was then approved by the mayor ands the City Council Speaker. The final process of holding the Commissioner's title did not happen in a few weeks, but a long process that took several months.

VAC Commissioners of New York City
Reference material from the VAC website: www.nyc.gov/html/vac

VAC is compromised of sixteen (16) Commissioners, nine (9) of whom are appointed and seven (7) of whom serve as ex-officio members, representing various governmental offices or bodies. All Commissioners serve without compensation.

The appointed Commissioners represent various groups that are under-represented in voter registration and voting, civil/voting rights organizations, disabled groups, public agencies and offices, and the business community. VAC's day-to-day operations are conducted by the Coordinator.

Three (3) Commissioners are appointed by the Mayor and six (6) are appointed by the New York City Council. The Mayoral and Council appointees are as follows:

Dr. Jeffrey F. Kraus, Chair – Professor of Political Science, Wagner College (Mayoral Appointee)
Ms. Jane Kalmus, Vice Chair – Executive Director, National Non-Partisan Voter Registration Campaign (Council Appointee – Manhattan)
Vacant – (Council Appointee – Bronx)
Ms. Loretta E. Prisco – Educator, Pace University (Council Appointee – Staten Island)
Mr. Morshed Alam – Department of Environmental Protection (Council Appointee – Queens)
Nayibe Nunez-Berger – Supervisor, Queens Family Court, Mental Health Services
Mr. Glen D. Magpantay – Staff Attorney, Asian American Legal Defense & Education Fund (Council Appointee – Citywide)
Robert J. McFeeley – (Mayoral Appointee – Staten Island)
Vacant – (Council Appointee – Brooklyn)
Seven (7) Commissioners serve as ex-officio members and they are as follows:
Hon. Carol Robles-Roman – Deputy Mayor for Legal Affairs
Marcus Cederqvist – Executive Director, Board of Election
Hon. Mark Page – Director, Office of Management and Budget
Hon. Frederick A.O. Schwarz – Chairman, NYC Campaign Finance Board
Hon. Betsy Gotbaum – Public Advocate

Hon. Michael A. Cardozo – Corporation Counsel, NYC Law Department
Hon. Joel I. Klein – Chancellor, NYC Department of Education

*   *   *   *

The Petitions Have to Be Technically Correct

I continue to encourage other immigrants to learn the political process, just as I had to learn it. After I ran for the state senate, some New American Democratic Club members started to run for elected offices. They were not always successful because they lacked the experience, exposure, and reputation that I had established over the years. They had not always taken the time or the effort to learn the process. Even if the elected office is not a high profile office, those who are seeking to be elected need to learn the process correctly.

When I ran the second time in the school board, I helped eight other immigrants to run, as part of our coalition. In my district, I was helping them to collect the signatures, writing the petition, binding their petitions (even the binding of the petition signatures has to be done a certain way), showing them how to challenge other candidates, and how to defend their petitions.

During my first and second campaign for the school board, Arthur Rojas and I were challenging other candidates. We used to knock out some candidates. I know now how to put my opponents into trouble: we found errors in their petitions that caused them to be taken off the ballot. As Arthur and I learned, we found reasons to eliminate the competition. The goal is to get rid of the competition in the beginning before someone can get on the ballot. For example, we challenged an opponent's names in a number of ways: the addresses were not right. There was writing over a signature or the petition was not bound right. The petition with its signatures is a serious business.

In 2006, I ran for the position of a local City Assemblyman. I spent $54,000 of campaign money to a consultant to get me on the ballot properly. My opponents included two district leaders and two state committeewomen. By looking at their petitions, three of them were eliminated from the ballot. They had done something technically wrong in their submissions. There are even certain rules and laws as to how the petitions are bound and two letters have to be part of the petitions. Candidates must have the help of someone who knows the laws and rules to meet the city and state requirements to be on ballot.

Lesson Number 1: If you do not know the rules of getting on a ballot and of knowing how to knock your opponents off the ballot, you will be wasting your money trying to run for office.

Every single part of the petition has a rule and regulation. If one item is not done properly, a candidate/opponent can be disqualified. After Arthur and I had submitted our petitions over the years to be on a ballot, we were always scared that somebody would find something wrong. It is very serious to have any mistakes on a ballot because if it can be proven that something was done illegally the candidate can go to jail.

If I want to disqualify my opponent, I can take his petition to court and challenge his signatures. Arthur and I have done that and won. We would ask the court to investigate how the signatures were collected. If they were obtained by falsifying the signatures, the person would be convicted of a felony.

If the court challenged a signature, I could not expect someone to take off from work to come into court to tell the judge that they did sign the petition. In this example, the signatures in that case are genuine, but it can be hard to prove the signatures are authentic if the person does not come to the court. If a doctor is running for office, he could be in serious trouble if he can not authenticate the signatures. The court could take away his license to practice medicine if the judge thought that he had collected signatures illegally. The need for accuracy is so critical because it can be so dangerous if a candidate is accused of illegal signatures.

Many politicians are under the microscope, not only by the media, but your opponents are going to give you a hard time in any way they can find. Thank God, Arthur and I always did everything correctly. Through it all, I learned and now I can help others and be a political consultant.

Lesson Number 2: If you want to run for office, do all the procedures correctly.

Over the years, I have met most of the New York City politicians and I like to call them all my friends. Some of my friends have suggested that I could take a political appointment. The problem with political appointments is that they may not last too long. Look at what happened with former Governor Eliot Spitzer. He lost his job, so all his people he appointed lost their positions. If I took a political appointment, I could lose my job if the political climate changes.

As for running for office, it is very, very tough. Democracy does work, but you have to know what you are doing if you want to run a campaign.

My Voter Assistance Commissioner position runs for six years. Those who take a commissioner's job do it for various reasons: political experience, power, and recognition for being part of the system. It is an unpaid job, so I'm doing this work as a Commissioner to help the city and to get people involved in politics and voting system. I still love politics, even though I can't always win every race.

Reprinted by permission from The Queens Courier

June 11, 2003

Teaching Fellow Immigrants How to Vote

BY JAMES FANELLI

Not many New Yorkers can boast flying to Bangladesh on Air Force One to tour the country with President Bill Clinton, nor can they showcase multiple proclamations from New York City commending them for exemplary civil service.

Morshed Alam, 45, an Bangladeshi immigrant who lives in Jamaica (Queens), can lay claim to such merits. They are a testament to the community work he has done for Bangladeshis and all immigrants, since he arrived in the city in 1984.

When Alam left his homeland, he was 26 and recently married. He and his wife, pregnant with their first child, wanted to escape their country's poor economy and abysmal political situation.

With the help of his brother-in-law, who already lived in America, they came to New York, where, according to Alam, 120,000 Bangladeshis now make their home in the greater metropolitan region. With his chemistry degree from the university in the Bangladesh's capital, Dhaka, Alam obtained work as a researcher for pharmaceutical companies in Manhattan. In 1990 he became a chemist for New York City's Environmental Protection Agency.

While he loved working to protect the environment, Alam held another passion—organizing a political voice for the under-represented—one embedded in him from his days in Bangladesh, where he participated in his country's war for independence from Pakistan in 1971 and its subsequent struggle for democracy.

Alam spent his formative years in Dhaka. During Bangladesh's struggle for independence, he delivered food and supplies to soldiers on the frontline. After it successfully seceded from Pakistan, the newborn country fell into a turbulent period of ineffective government and military coups. During his time, he was a student at the University of Dhaka, a political hotbed in the late 1970's and 80's. There, Alam became a nationally renowned student activist, leading demonstrations for democratic reform and pushing for an end to military rule.

When he left for America, he had he had accumulated a wealth of experience in organizing unheard voices and fighting for their right to vote, so it's not surprising he brought along this political acumen to his surrogate homeland.

Since settling in Jamaica, Alam has been a key figure in community politics, spiriting programs to get immigrants of all ethnicities to vote and voice their political opinions. In 1990, he founded the American Bangladeshi Friendship Association (ABFA), saying, "It was a way to address Bangladeshi issues and exchange ideas and opinions with different communities and groups."

The group holds programs and seminars on immigration politics and how to become a citizen and register to vote. It also connects Bangladeshis to other immigrant groups, by holding interfaith prayer services and sponsoring anti-bias forums.

Alam has also worked as a public servant, spending 12 years in the trenches of the most local politics: school boards. As a member of School Board 29, Alam says he had his most rewarding experiences. His proudest moment came when he and the other board members instituted a multi-cultural program, which offered after-school program for parents of different ethnicities to interact. It also ensured ESL classes and bilingual education, and it widened school cafeteria menus to represent foods from all ethnicities. Pointing to its effectiveness in bridging gaps, Alam said, "It's important to expose children to new cultures."

In 1998, the politically active Bangladeshi-American ran for State Senator against incumbent Frank Padavan, a public servant for over 30 years, who most challengers would be weak-kneed to face. To make the task more daunting, the Queens Democratic Party declined to endorse him.

Having survived beatings from state police in Bangladesh, Alam is no stranger to adversity, so when the Queens Democratic party nixed his endorsement he simply organized a new party, the New American Democratic Club. With its support, Alam finished with 40% of all votes. Though he lost the election, it was the largest percentage of votes any candidate had mustered against Padavan. The resilient, immigrant hasn't dismissed another election run, but he has no immediate plans.

"Somebody has to work as a bridge not just for those from Bangladesh, but for new and old communities," said Alam, a calm and pensive man with a lean frame.

His tireless work for immigrants has not gone unnoticed. In November of last year, Alam was named commissioner of the Voter Assistance Commission, a New York City agency that helps new Americans get involved in government and the political process through voter registration and education. "I am very outspoken about new communities," said Alam. "With more people coming here, they need more say."

Alam knows the importance of his commission, and the need to get immigrants to vote, from his own experiences in the city—not all of them rose-colored. He says the months after the September 11th attacks were especially tough. Native New Yorkers, both young and old, would come into his family's Laundromat business and inveigh hateful messages. "They would say, 'When are you going back to Afghanistan?'" said Alam, somewhat bemused since he has never been to the country. He notes regretfully that the ongoing war on terrorism and war in Iraq continue to spur hate crimes against Middle Eastern and South Asian immigrants in the community.

Alam says men attending the Jamaica Muslim Center have been attacked, and some students from these ethnic groups have been picked on at schools in Jamaica.

Though the incidents have been upsetting, they have not diminished his view of America as "the best democracy around." He attributes the tension to poor media coverage and the lack of dialogue between old and new communities. He also thinks that new immigrant groups need to do more to integrate themselves into American life. "A lot of Middle Easterners and South Asians are not involved in the mainstream community," observed Alam.

To undo the paucity in communication, Alam is doing what he always does, mobilizing communities. The ABFA has held many demonstrations since the World Trade Center disaster that spotlight hate crimes, including one recently in March attended by many local politicians.

Alam still misses his family and friends in Bangladesh and returns each year to visit them. He also wishes some of his native land's culture and customs would rub off on America. Alam recalls nostalgically how everyone in a 10-mile radius from his birthplace in Comilla-Chadpur knew each other. He doesn't see that communal living here in the states. This wistful memory may be the reason why Alam spends so much time bringing people together in his new homeland.

Reprinted by permission from India Abroad

January 3, 2003

Morshed Alam appointed to New York's Voter Assistance Commission

BY MOKIKA JOSHI

Social and political activist Morshed Alam has been appointed to the New York City Voter Assistance Commission—a government agency set up in 1988 to encourage voter registration and participation.

Ala, who migrated to the United States from Bangladesh and has lived in New York since 1984, was appointed by a unanimous vote November 20. His term ends June 30, 2004.

December 18, the city council presented him a proclamation recognizing the appointment. Council member John Liu, the first Asian Pacific American legislator in New York City, facilitated the process. City Council Speaker Gifford Miller and Council members Hiram Monserrate, James Gennaro and David Weprin were present.

"I feel proud," Alam told *India Abroad* before the ceremony at City Hall. "It is an honor for my work." Alam has been involved with various social and political organizations in Queens and New York City. "When I came to be a part of the country, from where on we can contribute to the community," he said.

In 1992, he founded the New Americans Democratic Club, envisaging it as a coalition of various communities—Hispanic, African-American and South Asian. "If you can work with other groups, you can be a power," he said.

In 1998, he ran for the New York State Senate on a Democratic ticket and received 42 percent of the vote against Senator Frank Padavan. For over 10 years her served as a member of the School Board 29. He set up the American-Bangladeshi Friendship Association, a civic organization in Queens that helped 9/11 victims' families access relief.

Alam worked with various immigrant groups and community leaders. "It is an interesting, educating and rewarding process," he said.

As part of the 16-member commission, the immediate task before him is to develop a good working relationship with all departments and commissioners, and to reach out to voters.

"Most voters are not registered. They don't understand its importance," he said. "This will be my priority."

Even though the South Asian community has been in the country for four decades, there is a lack of interest in the political process. Alam said this is because people don't understand the system. In Third World countries, politicians spend money to buy the people and entertain them, he said, whereas in the United States, people give money to politicians.

While politics in the Third World is seen as a way to get rich, in the US people have a clear picture of their finances before and after they are elected.

He urged people to become part of the neighborhood and the community. It is important to strengthen local politicians, because politics here is local, he said, "A President cannot do anything in the Council," he explained. "For that, you have to pass a Bill."

Alam said h was working at the grassroots level, trying to educate people about the importance of being involved. "Wherever we are, we should be a part of the community. School board, civic associations, block and district associations, labor unions, advocacy groups." on why the South Asian community, though active in fundraising, had not been able to gain much political visibility, Alam said it was one of several components in politics.

"They are not really organizing to be a power," he said. "They raise money for whom? President Clinton. George Bush. The Governor. But they are not raising money for any councilmen here."

Another aspect that the community prefers to do things for big people and get small favors in exchange, or be able to tell others that you know them, Alam said.

The governor has a responsibility, state-wise, and he can do very little for one small group, he said. For instance, in New Jersey, about 200,000 Indians out of 5 or 10 million people is a tiny percentage. But when people raise money for Council members, they can seek help when they have housing, immigration, health, or education-related problems.

"In this city, statistics show that 100,000 Indians vote. Believe it or not, going out and voting is 500 times more effective than 20 million dollars," he said.

CHAPTER 6

POLITICS IN GENERAL

A Rare Physical Attack

In 1993, I founded a civic group called American Bangladesh Friendship Association whose many goals included voter registration, voter education, medical help, citizenship drive, and connecting to other organizations that help with health, education, ESL, and housing.

I did experience an incident when I was personally attacked after a street fair I had helped to organize in Astoria when we were raising money for the Bangladesh community. The fair had ended in the afternoon, so I waited by my car with a friend because I had an appointment with the editor of a Bangladeshi newspaper at his office on Broadway and 34th Street.

As we talked, two Hispanic men in their early twenties were walking towards us. My friend was on my left, but they did not bother him. The two young men came straight to me. Without any warning, they punched me on both sides of my eyes. My glasses fell off and I fell unconscious in the street. My friend reported they said nothing, only laughed and walked away. They did not take anything from me.

The police came and an ambulance took me to the Elmhurst Hospital. From there, I asked to transferred me to the Long Island Jewish Hospital, which they did. The punches had fractured the bones under both eyes, resulting in my eyes turning black and blue and becoming swollen. The fractures took a long time to heal.

Why did they attack me for no reason? The prevalent theory had people believing that a group of political enemies were behind what happened because of any number of fears: my growing notoriety, my outspokenness about immigration issues, my opposition to fundamentalism, my statements against extremism, and anything I said that could upset the status quo. We assumed that some people could not accept my message of change and acceptance of one another. We had no proof, but it was assumed that a group of people hired the two young men to do it and timed it when a lot of people knew I would be at the event.

Mayor Dinkins's people called me and they called on the police to assist me with a prompt investigation. At that time, the Queens County party chairman was Congressman Tom Menton and the attack happened in his district. He also called and asked the detectives to assist me. They did come by, interviewed me, tried to find the young men, but basically the two attackers disappeared.

The attack got some attention when some newspapers wrote about extremism and what people do when they don't like someone. There will always be those who don't like to see change. Maybe some people feared I would change the established political system.

My suffering went beyond the pain of the physical attack. I paid the price for trying to be involved—I suffered the opposition from my own Bangladesh community and opposition from a group of Muslims. Even though I was trying to help the Muslim immigrants, certain fundamentalists thought I was doing something wrong by involving myself in American politics. It was not the whole Muslim community, but certain Muslims made it known they were upset with my efforts. Still, I would not allow their antagonism to stop me from getting involved in the system and the civic movement.

I found it interesting that some who opposed me were financially well off. They had the money to help me, but didn't. They probably had various personal reasons—maybe jealousy, my unexpected political and civic success, or they didn't like me getting so much media attention. When I sought financial help for my campaigns, most Bangladeshi people would not contribute. The local Bangladeshi newspaper even predicted that I would probably only get 2% of the votes and said openly that I did not know what I was doing. They were discouraging people from contributing to my efforts. I consoled myself by thinking I would at least be paving the way for other minority candidates in the future. Even when I ran for the school board elections, I did not get that much support from my own Bangladesh community. The truth is I got support from the community at large—my coworkers, those concerned for the immigrants, and those concerned with the local community issues. They turned out to be the ones who helped me.

Whenever I ran for office, I have also suffered the comments of plenty of naysayers—"It's impossible for him to win"; "He shouldn't run for office"; "He shouldn't be part of the system"; "Who is he to be running?"

Political involvement is not always an easy task. However, I can say in looking back that I did have a positive influence on a lot of different ethnic people in order to get them to run for an elected office.

*   *   *   *

The times are beginning to change when it comes to more Bangladeshi seeking political office. A group of Bangladeshi got together for a reception to honor a fellow Bangladeshi elected as a city council member in a small city in New Jersey. I know of more Bangladeshis who are now elected officials in New Jersey, Pennsylvania, upstate New York, and one state senator in Michigan. More Bangladeshi and other ethnic groups are calling me to ask, "How can I get involved? How can I get elected?" That is a complete turnaround of my own Bangladeshi people who opposed me when I started out.

Now, my Bangladeshi people realize that they made a mistake because they want to see their children involved in the community, which they see as including educational, civic, and political causes.

Since 1988, there has been a heavy influx of Bangladeshis coming to the U.S. because of a lottery visa. The U.S. gives 50,000 lottery visas for 70-80 countries in the world. That means about 10%-20% of the Bangladeshi people obtained those lotteries, allowing about 5,000 in every year. These are new Bangladesh immigrants who come in besides the other immigrant procedures of family or work sponsors.

My activity has not been confined to New York City alone. I have run for office in New York, but my political activity has been across the country among the Bangladesh, South Asia, and the immigrant communities. That has included visits to California, Georgia, Washington, D.C., and Michigan. My public speaking engagements have included Chicago, Boston, and Denver. My goal is to inspire others as they hear my story of political and civic involvement.

A New Attitude for Immigrants

The main problem I find among the immigrant community in New York City is that most of the people in these communities are poor. Most immigrants come here in search of new wealth. Their one and, sometimes, only interest is to make money. They don't think this is their country or that they should try to help this country to be better. They don't think that they have to give back something to America. That attitude is what I am trying to change.

My philosophy is to challenge them by saying, "Listen, we came here. Our children are going to be here. We are going to die here. Let's do something here. Let's do our part here." When I go around, I usually talk about the importance of making education better and why education is important. I try to show them that education is the light in the tunnel.

Some people tell me that they have a PhD degree, but I feel I am talking to some illiterate people because they have no concept and no interest in helping their communities, America, or their homeland. When well off people neglect what they can do to contribute to society, I look at that as a selfish attitude, despite whatever wealth they may have accumulated.

What Is My Political Future?

I have the feeling that I have come to a point where I cannot go further in my political career. I feel stuck in the same place. I am busy doing more organizing, but I don't know where my political future will take me.

The emotions of 9/11 certainly had a negative impact on my political career. First of all, I am a Muslim. My religion made a significant impact on my political future right away in what is mostly a Christian country. Other candidates use the religious card as a way to talk against me and to weaken my candidacy. When candidates see that they cannot discredit my candidacy in other ways, they will bring up the religious issue. Those opponents rely on the old tactic of what is called dirty politics, that is, trying to degrade and discredit the opponent by making hurtful and false statements. They do not focus on issues, but on the emotions they can illicit. Without a doubt, the events of 9/11 marked a turning point for me.

In 2006, I ran for the New York State Assembly in District 25, which had about a 50% immigrant population. I thought it possible to win. The election was held on September 13th. The five-year anniversary of 9/11 came along and it created a reminder of what certain Muslims extremists had done to this country. I found that I lost support even among the immigrant community because of the 9/11 issue.

People know that I am not a radical Muslim, that I am very fair, and that I strongly oppose Islamic fundamentalism and terrorism. As far back as July, 1993 I voiced my opposition against Islamic fundamentalism and terrorism in some South Asian communities. I was talking out against religious politics.

I am not blaming the American people for their attitudes, but now I know the impact of 9/11 on my life, besides damaging the world economy and trust. If I had been running for president, I know I would automatically have lost because my opponents would have brought up the Muslim-religious issue as a scare tactic for the voters. Barack Obama, the Democratic candidate for president, has had his share of detractors who have accused him of being a Muslim at one time. It's only necessary to scratch the religious surface lightly to cause a serious wound of suspicion in the minds of the voters and that suspicion can easily defeat a candidate. Unfortunately, today we live in a very suspicious world and people can be suspicious of the religious affiliation of their candidates.

*   *   *   *

Immigrants need to accommodate themselves to American culture. For example, women in business may have to give up wearing their native dress in order to wear a business suit. If a woman is running as a political candidate, she will have greater success in winning an election if she wears business clothes in order to look western. If an immigrant is a student, that student should be part of student activities, the student body, and student government. If an immigrant is a street vendor, he should be part of some street vendor association. If an immigrant is a taxi driver, he should be part of the taxi association. Wherever the immigrant finds himself, he or she should be part of the decision-making groups. Membership alone is not the goal. The membership allows a person to voice what should change in order to make improvements. The message is to learn to participate in America and to give back. This "give back" is also seen in political-civic participation.

Deal With Prejudice, Don't Let It Defeat You

Every immigrant has to realize that prejudice can and will happen. It is something that every immigrant who has an accent or a certain color has to deal with. Though there are hate laws in the United States, these laws cannot always control people from showing hate to others.

I fought for hate crime laws. After 9/11, I held a demonstration through my American Bangladesh Friendship Association against terrorism. We did a candlelight vigil in support of the victims of 9/11 and stated our opposition to terrorism. Also, I did a symposium against terrorism and organized a multi-religious dialogue. I gathered together some of the Imams. We discussed with them what they should tell the congregations about what is right and what is wrong. My view is that any mosque or any church should be places where people should solve their humanity issues and not only the place to pray.

Religious politics still plays into the voters' thinking, especially when they hear about more terrorist plots to set off bombs. It shows that religious institutions of all faiths have to take a bigger role to stop terrorism or our suspicions for one another will get out of control.

As sophisticated, scientific, and rational the western world tries to be, it is interesting to see that religion still plays a role in our thinking, prejudices, and voting. Most voters have not and probably never will get away from religion influences on their political views. For example, a conservative Republican, such as Bush, did seek the endorsement of Protestant Evangelicals as well as the Catholics, including the pope.

*   *   *   *

A political candidate has to work with a mosaic of issues: money, religion, ethnicity, and race. First of all, running for office takes a lot of money. It takes a lot of volunteers. You cannot do it by yourself. Even if a candidate has a lot of money to win an election, it may not happen, especially if an opponent plays dirty politics and brings up irrelevant, character-damaging issues.

A candidate has to be prepared to deal with religious competition (Christian, Jewish, and Muslim candidates). For myself, I look beyond religion because I have been a political consultant for candidates in various religions. I have helped a Jewish candidate run for office. I found the

Jewish community to be very strong and well organized. In addition, I respect how well organized the Christian and Jewish community members are and how well the know the system.

When I First Started Campaigning

I had two problems from my South Asia and Muslim communities: (1) some opposed me because they don't like to get involved in mainstream politics and (2) I am not a conservative Muslim as some would want me to be, just as some Christians like to support only conservative Christian candidates. I have found that it takes time to change people's attitudes, but attitudes can change.

As for my political future, I still feel I do not have the support of the Democratic machine for one fundamental reason right now. The machine wants the candidates to be loyal to whatever they say. The candidate cannot always make his own choices. For me, I have to say what is right and what is wrong.

I certainly hope that someday all candidates would get beyond the influences and controls of the lobbyists and do what is right for the people.

Reprinted by permission from The Queens Courier

Vol. 14, No. 26 November 12-18, 1998

Alam Loses But Proves His Point

BY NITZBURG ON POLITICS

Did you think that an unknown Bangladeshi immigrant could almost unseat one of the state's most powerful Republican State Senators? The Democratic Organization sure didn't think so, because they discouraged **Morshed Alam** from running, citing fears that Alam on the ticket meant political death to next-door Assemblywoman Ann-Margaret Carrozza. They needn't have worried. Carozza kept her Assembly seat, winning big. Padavan, for his part, didn't feel a threat and didn't campaign hard enough to make the difference for his long-time ally, Assembly candidate Doug Prescott. Was Alam crushed? Think again. Alam got 40.3 percent of the vote without much money, and most significantly, without any support or help from the powerful Democratic Organization. With help, Alam could have won. Cheers go for the two Democrats with guts enough to help Alam and defy the Backroom Boys – Councilman **Sheldon Leffler** and District Leader **Chet Szarejko**. "Congressman **Gary Ackerman's** endorsement also brought us to a new high, and we were really helped by the Sierra Club, the New Americans Dem Club and the endorsement of Senator **Daniel Patrick Moynihan**," said campaign manager **Arthur Rojas**. Most of the credit for a really good campaign goes to Alam and Rojas. Watch for both (and dozens of other political leaders drawn from the ranks of Queens' one million immigrants) to dominate Queens politics in the next generation.

October 14, 1997

Way Beyond the Melting Pot

New Americans and New York's New Ethnic Politics

BY ALISA SOLOMON

When the New Americans Democratic Club met in the Malabar Indian restaurant in the far reaches of Queens Village last week, the two dozen members squeezed around a long table resembled the UN cafeteria set more than the dealmakers of Tammy Hall. But under the glare of the fluorescent lights and a sign asserting "Liquor is strictly prohibited," the club members—from Pakistan, Haiti, Venezuela, Taiwan, Ghana, all corners of the globe—set about changing the face of the Democratic Party to better reflect, and to answer to, its changing constituency. Exit the wafting smoke of the power-brokering meetings of old. Enter the scent of curry spices. And kimchi. And red bean paste. And salsa.

The brainchild of Morshed Alam, a 40-year-old Bangladeshi immigrant long active in civic affairs, the new group aims, he says, "to bring new Americans into the political mainstream." The soft-spoken Alam talks dreamily about how the growing immigrant population will "one day make a difference." His feistier vice president, Arthur Rojas, a 29-year-old second-generation Colombian, outs it more bluntly: "Both parties haven't been welcoming to new Americans, and the climate has become poisoned by nativist rhetoric. They better wake up. We are going to be ready."

Indeed, while the pundits remain fixated on black-white battles within the Democratic Party, a new wave is building that could change the terms of New York politics as profoundly as when Jews and Italians took on the Yankees and Irish a century ago, and in turn, blacks and Puerto Ricans challenged *them*. What direction it ultimately will take is up for grabs: As new immigrants become increasingly politicized, will those who subscribe to the ethic of heaving on the old bootstraps ally themselves with the individualist credo of the Republicans? Will they identify with the silenced masses more traditionally drawn to the Democrats? Or might this wave even sweep away the moribund system, leaving a new, multiplicitous structure in its wake?

For the time being, Republican anti-immigration fury has answered those questions, especially on the national level. In the 1996 presidential election, Clinton won a whopping 71 per cent of Hispanic votes—a 16-point swing from 1992. And Clinton won a solid majority of Asian votes last year, well surpassing his earlier showing. In New York City, the numbers are even more compelling. Asians gave 75 per cent of their votes to Clinton—84 per cent if they were first-time (read: recently naturalized) voters. The anti-immigrant attack has provided a "collective politicizing experience," explains Chung-Wha Hong of the National Korean American Service and Education Consortium, fueling a new level of activism, of which the NADC is only one measure.

Washington and Albany haven't been able to ignore it. Alfonse D'Amato, for one, rallied behind the welfare bill and its provision to cut off SSI benefits to elderly and disabled immigrants when it was proposed last year. Now he's supporting the restoration of those benefits. As for state legislators, one immigrant-rights activist reports a perceptible shift in Albany. "It used to be, 'We'll forward your letter to your congressman, honey,'" she says, citing how state pols insisted they had nothing to do with immigrant affairs. "Now at least they'll give us a meeting."

City politics are tougher to interpret, and, as the NADC is learning, more difficult to rally around. Beyond breaking the glass ceiling in the party and opposing anti-immigrant legislation, the group's platform is yet to be hammered out. "We're still new," shrugs Pauline Chu, the club's Chinese second vice president, who was defeated last month in a bid for Flushing's city council seat. "We will need time to find our positions and strategies."

Still, it's the nitty-gritty business of City Hall that may matter most in the actual lives of immigrants: housing, education, health care, economic development, police brutality. And debating specific policies threatens to crack open the fault lines not yet apparent in the new coalition. What's most pressing? Breaks for the city's mom-and-pop businesses, 80 per cent of which, according to Sung Soo Kim of the Small Business Congress, are owned by people who are not native English speakers? Or enforcement of minimum wages for the vast numbers of immigrants toiling in sweatshops? Bilingual education? School vouchers? The NADC doesn't yet know. It is making no endorsement for mayor.

One reason for immigrants' political diffidence, explains Queens College anthropologist Roger Sanjek, is that "immigrants who came to New York after 1975—after the fiscal crisis—have seen nothing but shrinking public services. They have no history of expecting anything from government." Adds Angelo Falcon of the Institute for Puerto Rican Policy, "Even with Giuliani's support of immigrants, you still don't have any policy for city services for immigrants." No surprise that last time around immigrants were divided in the mayoral race. Since then, hundreds of thousands of immigrants in New York have become citizens and registered to vote. It's impossible to predict whether the anti-immigrant taint of the G.O.P., or the Louima case, will push those votes toward Ruth Messinger, but more locally, this influx can force a major shake-up. "You're looking at Assembly districts with upwards of 8,000 newly registered voters," explains Margie McHugh of the New York Immigration Coalition. "That's an entirely new bloc that incumbents have no inroads into."

Though the NADC has citywide aspirations, it's no accident that it originated in Queens, the most diverse county in America. So many new arrivals are streaming into the borough that the dearth of affordable housing is often cited as the number-one problem. The local schools and the borough's only public hospital, in Elmhurst, are increasingly stressed; only community activism saved the hospital from being privatized by the mayor.

Whether working through the Democratic Party can be as effective remains to be seen. So far, the county committee has paid scant attention. The district leadership remains almost entirely white. Nevertheless, the NADC, now about 60 members strong, hunkers down at Malabar. The meeting meanders over news of upcoming races. Volunteers are signed up, though there's no discussion of where the candidates stand on particular issues. They're Democrats, and this is the way, counsels Rojas, to "make a contribution to our party and a name for ourselves."

But after the formal adjournment, NADC members drop Robert's Rules, revert to first names, dish up some curry, and start talking turkey. Here's where they decry the overcrowded schools, the pothole-ridden streets. And they don't hesitate to note the delicious irony that they are sitting deep in the heart of the district of state senator Frank Padavan, author of the scathing anti-immigrant report "Our Teeming Shores." "He's been in office since before I was born," remarks Vishal Trivedi, 22, the club's youth organizer. "He's in for a surprise."

CHAPTER 7

THE FIRST NON-RESIDENT BANGLADESH CONFERENCE 2007, DHAKA

Background

The Conference was held at the Hotel Sheraton, Dhaka. The government of Bangladesh provided support and the Scholars Bangladesh Organization (scholarsbangladesh.com) organized the conference.

Sample Speakers

There were many speakers from various countries, but some speakers of note included:

Anwar Chowdhury, Ambassador of Great Britain to Bangladesh;

Dr. Kamal Hossain, Chair of the Session, and former Foreign Minister of Bangladesh

Honorable Hansen Clarke, Special Guest and State Senator from Michigan

Abdul Hasan Chowdhury, Moderator and Former State Minister of
  Foreign Affairs

* * * *

I was a noted speaker who came with the title Voter Assistance Commissioner, New York City. This is what I said in my speech.

Good Evening! My name is Morshed Alam. I am a Bangladeshi-American. The passport I carry is American, but everything about me has Bangladesh written all over. Though I have lived now for almost 24 years in the U.S., Bangla is still the language of my choice. I like rice with lentils more than any other food; and I prefer Tagore songs to any other brand or variety of music. In short, inside and out, I am a Bengali, and I don't find any contradiction in it with my American identity.

How is it possible? I recall Nobel Laureate Amartya Sen's remarks that he was Indian, British, and American, all at the same time, and found no contradiction in such multiple identities. In fact, in his book *Violence and Identity*, Professor Sen claims that "the same person can be, without any contradiction, an American citizen, of Caribbean origin, a Christian, a liberal, a woman, a vegetarian, a long-distance runner, a historian, a feminist, a heterosexual…." In other words, every one of us has multiple identities and prioritizing one identity over the others can result in a very simplistic understanding of the person and what he/she really represents.

I understand Dr. Sen and his thesis, but I would not put it forth to explain my own duality. Instead, let me tell you a little about myself and how my transformation came about. This, I hope, will show why being Americana and Bangladeshi at the same time is not a statement in contradiction. I chose to immigrate to the U.S. and to accept American citizenship primarily for the opportunity it offered me personally and the benefits that living in the United States afforded my family. I have made use of those opportunities and feel extremely thankful for the way I have progressed. But not for a moment have I abandoned my other identity – my Bangladeshi self. I am indebted to Bangladesh not only because it is the country of my birth and it is the place where my mother remains buried, but also because Bangladesh helped shape my world view. As a student at Dhaka University, I learned quickly to become a social and student rights activist. Those were my formative years, the years that made me conscious of my social and political reality and of the challenges it offered for transformation. In the U.S., though I took part in what   may be describe as mainstream politics, my primary interest involves promoting and advancing the rights and opportunities of fellow New Americans—those who came from Bangladesh and from other nations around the world. This is in fact an extension of my work in Dhaka that I started many years ago.

As an environmental scientist, I am responsible for securing the water quality for the residents of New York City. That's how I make my living. But the principal identity I present to most people is expressed through my involvement in public service. In Bangladesh, anyone running for an elective office is called a politician, and that may be   mostly a dirty word. In the U.S., the same vocation is called public service or public activism. This is considered to be a highly respected and worthy activity, one that has great social value and may ultimately lead to a political office. Whenever such rewards arrive, they are always the result of hard work and untold personal sacrifices. One chooses to take part in public service largely because he or she finds it a vehicle to make a contribution to the community to which he or she belongs. When a community thrives, one also benefits as a member of that same community. Of course, I don't mean this is only an altruistic affair. One expects to be rewarded, in small or large measures, but usually that's not the goal. At least, not the goal that I had set for myself when I decided to enter public service. That was about twenty years ago, when I joined the local Democratic Party's neighborhood club and began organizing local immigrant communities towards political empowerment.

My activities as a member led me into more responsible positions. I became Chairman of the Board of Directors and eventually President. The Democratic Club to which I belonged was considered to be a mainstream Democratic Organization. Several years later I formed my own New American Democratic Club, which was primarily a political vehicle to enroll immigrants and new Americans. Our immediate goals were to introduce these new members into a society which may have been perceived as threatening or incomprehensible. Our members were asked to participate in various activities that would lead them into realizing the American Dream, i.e. joining social, political and educational organizations, becoming members of community boards and civic associations, and encouraging them to learn the English language as an important aspect of assimilation. We emphasized the importance of obtaining educational opportunities for their children. I, myself, ran for my first public office and became a member of the local Board of Education. There I became a vice president and began to shape local educational policies aimed at helping the new Americans in my community. I also led the initiative to have Bengali introduced into the New York City school system. My position on the school board helped to obtain various jobs for members of my community. I also used the prominence of my school board position to lobby for recognition of the Bangladesh Independence and Victory Day throughout New York City.

My public activism gave me the opportunity to eventually place my name as a candidate for the important position of New York State Senate. It was difficult for any New American to get the full support of the Democratic Party Organization, the majority party in New York, but I persevered mainly on my own and with a political consultant and a few friends. I waged a campaign against a most powerful 24-year Republican incumbent. The results of the election were a huge surprise to all of the political leaders   and pundits of New York. To the shock of many seasoned politicians and power brokers, I garnered 42 % of the vote against a formidable and accomplished political veteran. This campaign gave me a great deal of credibility as well as visibility in the political arena.   High political and public officials gravitated toward my base and, let's be honest, almost overnight I became a celebrity. I was asked to join President Bill Clinton's entourage during his official visit to Bangladesh and India in 2000. During this visit to Dhaka, I met the Prime Minister of Bangladesh and high government officials and attended the State Dinner hosted by the President of Bangladesh.

Upon my return I was made a New York City Voter Assistance Commissioner. I received awards from the New York State Governor, Congressmen, Queens Borough President, and the NY City Comptroller. During this period, my professional career also advanced tremendously and I became a recipient of one of the best New York City Employees of the Year award for my professional achievements.

The USA is often described as a melting pot, where people from different parts of the world gather and slowly merge into a common American identity. Yet, most immigrant communities survive as

independent entities. In every society, wherever people compete for jobs
and social comfort, the real strength lies in numbers. As Bangladeshis, we
are still a minor immigrant community. Whatever the real number is, in the
broader context, Bangladeshis as a community still matter little. I realized
quite early on that the only way we would mark our presence in the
boarder social infrastructure in New York is through integrating ourselves
with the rest of the societal fabric. Clearly, irrespective of our ethnic,
religious or national identity, we are connected by a set of common
interests, such as jobs, professional training, community outreach, school
needs, and medical assistance. Using a common template defined by our
common community needs, I have encouraged Bangladeshis to join hands
with other South Asian immigrant communities, including India, Nepal, Sri
Lanka, and Pakistan. Consequently, our national identities have erased, and
a common community identity has emerged.

I have made use of this solidarity among South Asian immigrants to
improve their overall standing. I have taken steps to further consolidate
opportunities for fellow Bangladeshis and other new immigrants, and have
continued to encourage them to   become politically active. In fact, fellow
South Asians have actually followed my footsteps and sought various local
and national offices.

Voter registration is another very important aspect of my concern for
the political advancement of newly arrived immigrants. To this end, we
have conducted voter registration campaigns, community meetings
engaged in political/civic involvement, and introduced a pattern of
lobbying for important Bangladeshi interest in trade, conservation, and
other international issues. I also recognized early on that it is important to
give the Bangladeshi/American residents a clearer and more powerful
voice in the federal government. This realization led to the formation of the
Bangladeshi Congressional Caucus.

I have talked enough about my work with Bangladeshis in the U.S.
But how does this work contribute to Bangladesh? In fact, my ability to
contribute to Bangladesh is proportionally dependent on my success as an
American. First, everything I do in America is inevitably linked to my
Bangladeshi identity. When *The New York Times* carried a front-page
article about my run for the New York State Senate, it identified me as an
immigrant from Bangladesh. When I almost toppled a New York

Republican Party icon in a statewide election, major networks focused on my background as a Bangladeshi. In other words, my success—whatever it is—contributes to improving Bangladesh's image. It helps change the conversation about Bangladesh, a country perennially described as poor and under-developed. When they read about me—and other successful Bangladeshi-Americans—they realize the story of Bangladesh is not one dimensional. We as a people are much greater than just the stereotype caricatured in the media.

Recently, I was asked about Bangladesh's image problem and what could be done to improve it in the West. My answer to my fellow Bangladeshi-Americans is always the same: "Prove that you are the best in your profession, whatever it might be." By proving that you are honest, hardworking, and useful to the community where you live, you prove your value and, in doing so, you raise the profile of your country of origin. If you are a taxi driver, prove that no one in New York can do this job better than you do. In fact, Bangladeshi taxi drivers have already proven that they are not just the very best in their profession, but are also outstanding citizens. You must have read about a Bangladesh cabbie who found a million dollars worth of diamonds in his taxi. He literally chased the rightful owner and handed over her property. The Mayor of New York City held a special press conference to hail him for his honesty and to thank him for being a model New Yorker. Yes, he was a single taxi driver, who happened to be from Bangladesh, who single-handedly changed a conversation about Bangladesh. Each time his story was flashed on the TV screens, every news outlet in the city repeated the word Bangladesh.

As I look back on the long path that I have traveled, two snapshots stand out in my memory. One from my childhood, when as a third grader, I was chosen the class captain. It gave me the realization that as a leader, even as young as a third grader, I can have enormous impact on other people's lives. The second snapshot is from my 2000 trip to Dhaka with President Clinton. How did that third grader from a poor, under-developed country, end up in Bangabhaban, laughing and chatting with arguably the most powerful man on earth? The answer: everything happens when you follow a dream and work had to realize it.

Thank you.

CHAPTER 8

MY PHILOSOPHY

My efforts in American politics over the years have shown to me that to win an election takes a great effort and a great many sacrifices. The highlights of some of my experiences include:

- Being elected twice as a New York City School Board member.
- In my first New York State senate race, I got 42% of the votes.
- In my second New York State senate race, I withdrew because I could not raise the $100,000-$200,000 necessary to finance my campaign in order to beat my opponent.
- In 2000, I attempted to run for city council, but withdrew because I did not have the necessary money: $100,000-$200,000.
- I have experience with organizing my own election campaigns. Also, I have worked as a volunteer for many elected officials in their campaigns.

When you run for office, you will discover those who support you, those who oppose you, and those who threaten you. What follows are some guidelines of what I have done and what will help you to preparing a political campaign.

Lesson 1: Get help from a variety of activists and leaders.
When I was running for state senate, I got a lot of help from different people and groups: Chet Szarejko, a district leader, state committeeman, and a famous activist in New York City; Doctor Farouque Khan, a famous

117

Muslim activist on Long island; and leaders in the Bangladesh, Chinese-American, Korean, Philippine, Hispanic, African-American, and West Indies communities. A wide variety of politicians helped me as well. For the most part, the Democratic Party did not oppose me, but I could not get them to support me.

Lesson 2: Build a coalition of many different neighborhoods and ethnic communities.

I built a huge network coalition among all the different immigrant communities.

Lesson 3: Be prepared to do as much as possible on your own without other volunteers.

Many times I had to do everything—Petitioning, campaigning, election day work, printing, and distributing palm cards that gives the slate information—without the party's help and with only my family helping me.

Lesson 4: Threats and negative publicity may be discreet or very direct.

Some people threatened me because they did not want me to take away votes from their candidates. If I gave in to the threats, I knew I would end my political life. Some newspapers and elected officials were telling me, "Don't run for that office. There is no reason. It is useless." There were those who were deliberately trying to undermine my candidacy in order to insure that their candidate would win. I have experienced what it means to be the underdog.

When I was running for the state senate the second time, the Democratic Party had a candidate. They wanted me to withdraw and support him. They said they would help me, but they did not do anything for me. I did withdraw, but for financial reasons. The Democratic candidate ended up only getting 36% and he had spent about $500,000. If the party had supported me with that kind of money, I could have won. I had a strong coalition of voters.

118

Lesson 5: The party that you belong to may not support you as a candidate.

When I ran for the city council election in 2000, all my attempts to run were not being supported. I wanted to represent the immigrant communities, which had very little or no representation. I tried to prove that the immigrants needed representation. Unfortunately, immigrants do not have the money or the commitment to support their candidate.

I used to spend 60-70 hours a week attending and organizing community meetings, community board meetings, city council meetings, block association, union, and environmental and advocacy group meetings. I was trying to give a message that we needed representation, we need to share the power, and we need to bring all the people together. I would gently remind the immigrants that they should not be sleeping when it comes time getting involved politically because the wrong candidate could create new laws that would hurt them and their rights. I always attempted to help others selflessly. Sometimes, I was successful and, sometimes, I was not.

Lesson 6: Results do pay off over the years.

I am proud to say that the Bangladesh community has come onto the political map in New York City because of my name, my presence, my participation, and my activism. When my name comes up, my old country name of Bangladesh often comes up too.

I am an established leader and political player in the immigrant community in New York City and in Queens because I'm constantly organizing at events and talking about the issues. The immigrant community is, sometimes, discriminated against because of their language, color, or ethnicity. They may be harassed and become target groups. Often, they do not know how to complain to the police, are afraid to complain, or don't know where to go to get help. As the ethnic groups and immigrants get politically involved, I have seen them make progress in protecting their rights and get the attention they need from the politicians.

Lesson 7: Immigrants need to learn the process.

It is all about the process of learning about the new country and how to be part of this new country. It is a process I am trying to teach to the people and encourage them to be part of. There is no better alternative than to grow in this society and be part of America. The country offers a huge opportunity for everyone. Nobody should blame anybody else. Nobody is inferior. With your have talents, commitment, and patience, you can achieve whatever you want.

When it comes to helping people and philanthropy, America offers a lot of help to the immigrants, if they participate. For the most part, Americans enjoy helping others, but you have to ask for the help in the right way.

In my campaigns, I tried to bring together the new immigrants and the citizens who were established. There is a gap between the two groups— new immigrants and the established citizens—because of a lack of information, besides the obvious differences of our cultures and views.

There are always some people who see negative trends. They may get discouraged and leave politics. That is the wrong thing to do—to give up. Politics is not always easy, but you can keep giving out a message. You can run for any elected office, but you have to know the system. If a person works as a volunteer, that person can help to educate the candidate as to what he or she should do for his community. You can bring to them any issue. You can bring a message. You can be a bridge between the community and the candidate. There are all different levels of people representing the community—city council members, state senators, community boards, US senators and congressmen. If you want to be part of helping society, helping candidates during the election is one of the processes.

Even though I lost in some elections, I still had given out my strong message: that nobody should deny rights to or be hateful towards the immigrant community or immigrant issues. I presented an important message—that we can all work together.

I brought a new dimension into politics. I see a lot of new people encouraged to try to run for political office as they follow my example and learn from me. I see more immigrant people taking jobs in government. I believe more and more immigrants are beginning to take a greater interest in government and aspire to be part of the system. I see these as more recent developments than when I first started. I believe my work has been as a catalyst to stimulate people to participate more and more in society.

*　　*　　*　　*

Although there is separation of church and state, it has to be said that religion, especially in the churches, does play a role in politics. It can be said that the churches are usually involved with politics and the candidates. When I was running for the school board in south Jamaica, I saw all the African American churches very involved with their candidates. I visited these churches who had to help those with low incomes, the less educated, and people who had a lot of anger and frustration from years of oppression. The churches I saw offered the masses a hope. They have excellent ways to deal with the people's frustrations. African-American churches became very important to me when I was campaigning. The good thing about African-American churches is that they present a message of hope.

I have found for the most part that the mosques are not significantly involved with politics. At the mosques, the Hindu temples, and even some of the Hispanic churches, I did not see that they were providing any messages to their members.

I was impressed how the churches play an important role in elections and in charity work.
The African-American churches act more as activists. Activism should not be a problem for the mosques, but for some reason they need to learn, to be educated, and to get more training about activism. They have to understand the American system. They have to learn that they can serve God by also helping the community.

Because of my achievements, I was invited to speak to police officers at John Jay College of Criminal Justice in Manhattan. I was giving a speech about cultural sensitivity. At another time, I spoke at Columbia University in the African-America Studies Department about voting rights and political participation from my perspective as a Voter Assistance Commissioner. Also, I spoke at Queens College a couple of times for different student organizations, such as the Department of Asian-Americans about my experience with politics.

When I was running as a candidate, one Muslim group on Staten Island invited me to speak. I gave the speech. When I came out to the parking lot to my car, I wondered why one young man followed me.

He came up to me and said, "Gentleman, I want to talk to you."

"What?" I asked.

"Who told you to do that politics?"

"Nobody told me. It's activism that I am doing."

"It's illegal according to Sharie, according to Islamic law."

"What?"

"You shouldn't do it."

I thought he intended to beat me, so I became afraid. I quickly got in, locked my car door, and drove away.

Twice I faced this type of attitude. Some Muslims don't believe it is right to participate in the system. This kind of attitude is discouraging. There are a few who like to yell at me and insult me. That happened only a couple of times. I believe that in the last ten years people are learning. Now, I don't see such blatant opposition. When I first started, I got a lot more opposition, insults, and threats.

My running is not just about me gaining an elected office. It is about helping my immigrant community learn to be involved—and that it is not wrong what I am doing. My community is learning. I think it is a tremendous achievement if I can help other immigrants become politically involved. I feel good about those accomplishments.

There are some Muslims who do not want activism, but would rather have a country run by the clerics. From my personal experience,

Bangladesh has a majority Muslim population, but the clerics do not control the government as they do in Iran. I believe that Bangladesh shows how Islam and democracy can work together.

As more people get involved with the American system, they will learn about their rights and not remain in an "isolationist attitude" within America that I have seen all too often. Those who do not know the American system will inevitably have misconceptions about politics and America.

Nobody pushes me to do what I do. After years of activism, I have lost some of my health, spent my own money, and exerted a lot of energy. I typically spent 60-70 hours a week involved in the community issues and politics—something I did for 17 years, seven days a week bringing people together and leading demonstrations. You name it, I tried to be there. I used to go to work at six o'clock in the morning. I would be back home at two o'clock to take a shower and then go out to all the meetings.

I never tried to push one religion. I looked at the human point of view. If a group of people expressed a need, I was there to try to help them.

I know some rich people, but they are not involved in helping others. They just make money and look to enjoy their lives. They have never done anything for their communities, for America, or for their home country. To me, that's selfishness. They are very smart in their professional life. But they are not smart enough to understand that they have to give back. They do not understand the satisfaction they can get helping others. They don't care to leave some special charitable work behind. It's not enough to say I have a store or I am a doctor. It's important to be able to say I have helped others. This is the difference of opinion between me and others. There are those who only want to look at having a big car and millions in the bank, but are "bankrupt" in doing good for others.

I differ with those people because I believe we all have to give back something good in our lives. We have to help other humans. It's not enough to do for yourself or your family. We are all part of the bigger

123

family. I know plenty of immigrants who only think they are here to make money and to keep as much money as possible for themselves. They need to have a new change of heart and mind. That is just a part of what I am pushing.

*   *   *   *

I still have much to do to get out the message about getting involved. It's easy for people just to ignore issues. I have the feeling that the second generation in immigrant families are not always that involved with the system too. I see all too often that everybody wants to get something from the system, but they do not always want to contribute back to society.

I remember a poster that said: vote or die. If you don't vote, you should not complain about what goes on. If you don't vote, you are not part of the system. You are paying taxes automatically, whether you vote or not, so I tell people they should vote; they should do something good for their communities; and they should do something good for their home countries. Doing good to help others is a great thing.

My philosophy is that the world is for a few days, that is, we live but a short time. What is so important is to leave behind some good. Life is not about money, money, money. Money cannot be the solution to everything. Money is only a small fraction of our lives, but it is not the complete solution.

*   *   *   *

New York City has the largest Bangladesh community in the U.S., then comes Los Angeles, and then Michigan. For example, the Bangladesh community in Detroit is between 30,000-40,000. Other Bangladesh communities can be found in Washington, D.C. and Atlanta.

In America, I have seen Bangladesh and Pakistani people living together in harmony, even though Bangladeshi people did go to war to secure their own country against Pakistan. I don't think people here want to relive what happened. My focus personally now is to bring everybody together. The idea is to bring the community together. The idea of community in America should not have to focus on race, religion, or skin color. When we were born, we didn't have any idea about differences. We had no concept of a country. We were born as human beings. Children are able to learn to play together, if the adults teach them to be tolerant and to show respect to everyone. My message is the same as that of the American Constitution and the Bill of Rights—to life, liberty, and the pursuit of happiness despite our differences.

There is a fact that cannot be changed at this moment: Bangladesh is a Third World country. Improvements are being made in the country, but very slowly. Education is making some improvements. Children are supposed to go to school in Bangladesh, but the law is not completely enforced. Such conditions in Bangladesh and around the world remind me that there is so much work to be done to help others.

*   *   *   *

In 2006, I ran for New York State Assemblyman. I lost in the primary. I have to admit that I got a lot of help from my union—the New York City Municipal Union. It has 125,000 active members and 50,000 retirees. They helped me, supported me, gave to my campaign money, gave me volunteers, and ran my office for about six months. I got an endorsement from District 1707 of the Employees Health Union. I got help from the national union AFSCME—the American Federation of the State, County and Municipal Employees. I got a lot of support from trade union members: Local 371, Local 375, Local 372, and Local 1407. Also, my Bangladesh, Indian, and Pakistan communities helped me.

As part of the process, I sent a letter to the different screening boards to introduce myself and my candidacy. When they accepted me, then I got an endorsement. I have been a union member for several decades. From 1997-2000, I served as president of one of the union chapters. Over the years, I have maintained a strong involvement with my union and other unions.

From 1992 to the present, I have been a delegate to Union 375, Technical Guild. I'm proud to be an activist and I still work closely with them. One of my good friends, Maf Misbahuddin, a union member, has been my big supporter. He is a fellow Bangladeshi and the treasurer of District 37, the second most powerful position in the union. To show that this can be a small world, Mark and I were fellow classmates in Bangladesh.

*   *   *   *

I still have lingering frustrations with the immigrants. When I go to civic associations, community boards, school board, Democratic clubs, Republican clubs, and other activist meetings, I feel discouraged because I do not see as many immigrants as I would like. Even in the highly populated immigrant communities of Jackson Heights, Woodside, Sunnyside, Brooklyn, and Bronx, the civic associations may only have 1% immigrant representation. It's the old community leaders who are involved in the meetings. I give them credit for being involved. Those who are young and came into the community need to be at the meetings to talk about their issues, but they are absent. Their absence and lack of interest remain as my biggest frustrations.

Young people are totally absent. Of course, some may be pursuing their professional life and going to college on their free time to double-up their skills. I understand they can be pressed for time, but they should not forget that the politicians will be affecting their lives for good or bad.

I find the 2008 Presidential campaign to be good because it is encouraging younger people to get involved with the candidates and the election. I hope to see the young people continue their participation with the same zealous spirit as time goes on. Then I will consider the 2008 campaign to have been successful.

Reprinted by permission from the Public Employee Press

Clean Water Proclamations

BY GREGORY M. HEIRES
DC 37, AFSCME, AFL-CIO

A chemist by trade, Local 375 member Morshed Alam is an environmentalist in practice.

As a quality Assurance Specialist at the Dept. of Environmental Protection, Alam ensures that the wastewater from sewage treatment plants doesn't pollute the city's waterways.

"When we treat wastewater and expel it to the river, it's almost as clean as drinking water. If we didn't do this, New York City wouldn't be a good place to live," said Alam, who is responsible for quality control at the department's 22 sewage treatment plant laboratories.

Alam worked as a chemist at a pharmaceutical company for eight years before he left the private sector for public service with DEP in 1992. "I love my job and feel very privileged serving the people of New York City," said Alam, a former Local 375 chapter president.

Protecting the environment

At DEP, Alam quickly distinguished himself as a conscientious worker dedicated to the department's mission of protecting the environment. He wrote a quality control manual and came up with standard operating procedures.

In addition, he set up a program to eliminate mercury thermometers from the laboratories. Potentially cancer-causing, mercury poses a health threat to workers. Now, DEP uses alcohol-based thermometers in the labs.

Alam was among nine DC 37 members honored in (December in the 100 Year Association of New York).

Outside of work, Alam continues to fulfill his public service ethos by throwing himself into community and political activities. A few years ago,

128

he ran unsuccessfully with the support of Local 375 for a state Senate position representing Queens.

A native of Bangladesh, he is active in immigrant issues. He founded the American Bangladesh Friendship Association, which helped people affected by the (/11 attacks and now assists immigrants in finding jobs and helps victims of domestic violence.

Alam, who came to the United States in 1984, serves as executive director of the New Americans Democratic Organization of New York State, which helps new citizens get involved in political activities.

The group also is pressing for legislation to permit permanent resident immigrants to vote in mayoral and city council elections.

"Those who have permanent status and are paying taxes should have the right to vote," said Alam.

CHAPTER 9

CONSULTANT TO INTERNATIONAL WORK

Perspective of Democracy in Bangladesh and India
America likes to claim it is the best democracy in the world, but it does not
have a good turnout of voters during elections compared to other countries.
In India, where about 50% of the people are educated and about 50% are
illiterate, the voting turnout is reported to be over 80%, while America
usually has about a 40%-50% voter turnout at the most.

Having made many friends in America who are from India and
Pakistan and from having grown up in the Southeast Asia region, I am
familiar with these other governments. When it comes to the practice of
democracy, India has some interesting differences from American
democracy.

The Prime Minister of India is elected by the people, while India's
Parliament selects the president, as stated in their Constitution. Since India
is 80% Hindu and 20% Muslim and other religions, Parliament does not
always choose a Hindu president in respect to the other minorities. That is
unique to India.

The current president Pratibha Devi Singh Patil is the first woman
president of India. Before her, India's Parliament picked a nuclear scientist,

a Muslim, and before him they picked a Hindu. Parliament even picked someone from the caste system and made him president.

India had a woman Prime Minister, Indira Ghandi, India's first and only female Prime Minister who served in three consecutive terms from 1966 to 1977 and was assassinated in 1984. She had come into power some 48 years before Senator Hillary Clinton even tried to be the first female presidential nominee. That was unique to India.

India's type of government is usually a coalition of 2-3 parties. At one time, they had a ten-party alliance. Now, they have the Communist Party, Socialist Party, and the Congress (something like a Social Democrat). The Socialists and Communist participate in the elections, even though they may not believe too much in democracy. Still, they cooperate. For example, the Prime Minister is from the Democratic Party and the Speaker is from the Communist Party. The government ministers are also a mix from different parties.

Although the people of India speak 56 different languages, the state language of India is Hindi. Their economy is booming and one of the most vibrant economies in the world, similar to those of China and Brazil.

Unfortunately, the caste system in India has to be recognized as undemocratic because it is discriminatory. This system was not created by the people of India by choice, but created during British colonialism as a way to rule the people. The British designed one group to rule another group by giving preferential titles to those who were more loyal to them, which became known as chadray. The title would make the person special in the community and society and it was mostly based on wealth, education, and a special symbiotic relationship the British had with certain Indians. Even though a British invention, the caste system has been part of society and the government for so long that it will take a long time to remove it, but there is a slowness and little motivation to dismantle it, leaving the low-caste Hindus not part of the government or the power system. Still, I find India a wonderful nation and its people motivated to get educated and eager to join the middle-class and be prosperous.

India has good relations with Bangladesh. India helped Bangladesh during its civil war with Pakistan in 1971. At the end of the Liberation War, about 20 million Bangladesh people had fled into India for protection where they stayed for more than a year. India gave them full support of shelter, food, and medical help. Also, the Indian Army supported Bangladesh and fought together with the Bangladeshi freedom fighters. I understand about 15,000 India soldiers were killed fighting in our Liberation War, so Bangladesh owes its gratitude to the Indian people for their great human sacrifice of soldiers who died and for their humanitarian efforts that helped millions of Bangladeshis who were in desperate need and facing starvation.

Bangladesh has wonderful relationships with its neighboring countries and those throughout Southeast Asia, including China. Even though Bangladesh is a struggling democracy and not wealthy, the country is important because of its location at a strategic location on the Indian Subcontinent.

On the other hand, India is growing at a phenomenal rate and is no longer just a regional power, but an international power. It conducts a large amount of business in Europe and has been expanding its trade interests in South America. In addition, India has been helping African countries to develop their economies and export their oil, and has been sending workers to Africa to help extract their minerals, ore, and natural resources.

To show how India has been eagerly extending itself throughout the world, a 2008 newspaper photo showed Pratibha Devi Singh Patil, India's female president, reviewing a Mexican Honor Guard in Mexico City. She came there because India and Mexico had signed a joint agreement on civil aviation. From Mexico, she would be continuing a 13-nation tour to South America.

Bangladesh is not at the stage where it can compete with India in the international markets, but I expect it will happen one day as Bangladesh strives to improve its economy. The government continues to improve international relations with other countries. One thing unique about Bangladesh is that it has about 150 million people. That's a large human resource. The country's opportunities for imports and exports will keep growing in such a large country, especially when its citizens become better educated and offer more services to other countries.

Bangladesh has a lot of resources. Americans may not know it, but Bangladesh exports 7% of its garments to America. Their other exports include quality tea, fish, and shrimp. With its many rivers, the country has a lot of fish to export, besides exporting harvested fish. In addition to America, the country exports to the Middle East, Malaysia, and South Korea. Products are not the only thing exported. There are about 5 million Bangladeshis working in the Middle East and South Korea in hotels and the construction industries. One of my agendas in consulting has to do with the human rights issues. As people go to these other countries, a host of new problems are resulting: new problems are created about housing and fair treatment; many labor disputes have arisen; and so many human rights issues about personal freedoms arise.

*   *   *   *

Following the lead of India and some other countries, my hope and personal goal is to one day see 70%-80% of the American voters participating in the elections. Why does India and Bangladesh get such a high turnout at elections? I think the people respect their opportunity to vote. India historically has been a poor country. The people realize they have only one thing—they have social power. That power comes through participating in the elections.

As an activist in America, I am accustomed to going to civic association meetings, block association meetings, trade union meetings, and advocacy group meetings. I feel that the young, the well-off, and the very poor are three groups who for their own reasons have not been motivated to vote or are not interested in politics. Those who are well-off have what they need and those who are very poor may feel disenfranchised from politics. As for those in India, most of the people still need a lot more. Therefore, they think the only way to make a difference is to participate by voting.

America is such a wealthy country that it may have lost respect for those who are poor and needy. The government does give out food stamps and other services to keep people from starving, but the poor and less fortunate in America can feel isolated from the social mainstream and do not see that voting will improve their lives.

Since coming to America, I have loved being involved in America's politics, civic life, educational system, and the labor movement. My priority has been to get more people involved in politics and making a difference in their communities.

Slowly, there are more South East Asians getting involved in American politics. One who has achieved an historic accomplishment is Bobby Jindal who on October 20, 2007 was elected the governor of Louisiana, becoming the first Indian American governor in U.S. history and the first non-white since Reconstruction. He resigned his seat in Congress in order to become governor. Born in Baton Rouge, Louisiana in 1971 and as a Republican, some people began proposing that he could be the Vice President candidate to run with Senator John McCain in the 2008 election. More interesting information can be found about Governor Jindal on the Internet. It would be quite an achievement if some day America has an Indian-American or a Bangladesh American as a Vice President or a President. In fact, there are any number of Southeast Asians and even Bangladesh Americans who are being elected into office.

* * * *

Honored for My Achievements
Over the years, I have had the unique opportunity to learn both the Bangladesh and the American system of politics—how to lobby, who to

talk to, the electoral system, and networking with the power players. My contacts have led to my establishing excellent relationships with all the elected officials of New York, including the governor, the New York City mayors, members of Congress, and New York's two U.S. Senators. By knowing these players, I know how to approach them and how to get things done. In addition, I have already been using my capabilities as a political consultant for some local New York campaigns.

If time and circumstances do not allow me to become a state senator or hold some other elected office, I do not feel I have failed. In many ways, my work as a political or civic lobbyist or consultant can prove very effective in making changes by my influencing those elected officials and other groups. I know I can help the immigrant community, the Bangladesh community, and American businesses through my contacts and without having to be elected.

Being an elected official is a commitment to the public in one area. As a consultant, I can help many groups. Since I have established a name recognition throughout New York City and the state, the elected officials, trade unions, and business people know me and I know how to approach them.

In 1994, the Governor Mario Cuomo of New York State declared March 26th as a commemorative day for New York State to recognize Bangladesh's independence, one of my achievements in helping to give recognition to that country, just as I have gotten recognition for other communities too.

When I was on the school board, the issue came up about what second languages should be taught. I advocated for Bangalese, my language, then Punjaabi, and Hindi as second languages in the New York School system, and those languages were added as I had requested. I have learned what it takes to make accomplishments in the system—about how to approach, when to approach, why to approach, and who to approach.

Some of my expanding interests have included helping Bangladesh to secure American and other foreign investors. Bangladesh has a lot of mineral resources, a huge gas reserve, quality coal, and oil, but the oil requires offshore drilling in the Bay of Bengal.

Although my focus has been local politics, I have developed making national contacts. I can see the time coming soon that my work will be more and more on the international scale as I help import-export companies in America, Bangladesh, and the South Asia region.

My contacts in Bangladesh are extensive. In fact, the president of Bangladesh was at one time my teacher. I'm in contact with a host of important people in Bangladesh: the former Prime Minister; I know all the senior ministers personally; I have connections with all the intellectuals; I know 60-70 members of Parliament; I keep in touch with about 60% of those aspiring to political office. I'm connected to many of those who are high level contacts in the country. If anybody or any company needs any help from the government, I am happy and confident that I can help them.

When I visited Bangladesh in 2007, I met with Bangladesh's President, Dr. Iaz Uddin, in his house where we had dinner. I shared with him *Crossing the Boulevard* which features my wife and I as one of the immigrants mentioned in the book. When he asked to keep it, I gave him the copy. In our custom, the teacher and student are like father and son. That is the kind of respect we have for each other. He wanted to show some of his other "children" the success of his student Morshed Alam.

While visiting, I met with Dr. S.M. Faiz, the Vice Chancellor of Dhaka University. This is the oldest university in Bangladesh with about 40,000 students and is called "the Oxford of the East." That is a respectful way of saying it is the best university in the country. Dr. S.M. Faiz was also one of my teachers. He wanted to see me and to hear of my success in America. We were very happy to see each other and very proud of our association. He took me around the university to show the changes at the university since my graduation from there more than 25 years ago. As an interesting coincidence, he, too, had been a student of the Bangladesh president, Dr. Iaz Uddin.

During that visit, one of my former teachers, who has since become the Vice Chancellor of Call Open University of Bangladesh, presided at a reception given to me. I was thrilled to have him host the event because we respect our teachers almost as if they are gods, so it is a high honor to have a former professor give me honorable recognition. My former professors represent the highest qualified teachers in the country and, likewise, they are teaching the best qualified students in Bangladesh. Receiving their accolades made me feel that my life had been successful, even though I had not achieved great wealth. The respect they gave me was worth more than money.

Although I have had my disappointments, such as not winning the state senate position, I look on what happened as not meant to be. When someone tells me my experiences and contacts are worth a million dollars, I don't think about the money. I find it more important in my heart to be of help to those who are less fortunate.

In the United States, we don't see thousands of people starving, but some immigrants have seen those conditions in their country. Millions of people die every year due to the scarcity of food, lack of minimum medical care, poor sanitation. Some people may only eat once every three days. Some people die because they don't have saline (salt) water to protect them from losing electrolytes. If people have an upset stomach or diarrhea, a common ailment in Africa, Middle East, and Asia, they can die. For as little as fifty cents a day, someone's life could be saved. There are immigrants who have become successful business people and professionals in America and who have enough money to help those suffering back in their home countries. I want to do something to inspire those immigrants to give back to their homelands.

*　*　*　*

The other day the former president of the Jackson Heights Indian Business Association, V. M. Ghandi, called to ask me, "Do you know the editor of *India Abroad*, Razu Gopal, passed away?"

Gopal had become very famous as the owner, publisher, and editor of the foremost newspaper of India abroad. He passed away at the age of 80. I had met with Gopal three months ago at which time he said, "I have not seen you for a long time. Give me your card." I gave him my card. He was involved with the NRI—Non-resident Indians. They have a convention every year in India and he had been one of the honorees in 2007. He said, "I want to write something about you." I asked, "What is that?" He said, "What you went through. What is going on with you. I want to write and then people can learn more from your experiences as an activist."

In the days before the call, I had been thinking about him when suddenly I got the call. I remember him telling me that he never wanted his passing put in the newspaper. His instructions were that there would be no memorial ceremony and no flowers. Two days before he died, he said to someone, "Nothing to nothing. Let me go. If anybody really loves me, contribute money to my foundation."

Mr. Gopal's foundation provides a lot of help to Indian youth. One is the internship program the foundation sponsors for youth who come from India to be interns in Washington, D.C. The internship teaches them about the American system and how to get a job in America in the political system.

I was shocked and sad to learn of his death. As someone from South Asia, he supported my efforts in his newspaper. I appreciated his help over the years because his newspaper is one of the most influential papers in the immigrant community.

I recently began a foundation in Bangladesh in the name of my parents—Abdus Samad Munshi-Azizneesa Trust Foundation. It is registered only in Bangladesh where it will be providing educational grants to needy children and operating free medical clinics that will serve about 150 people a day. As part of the next phase of my life, I see myself involved in three main endeavors: (1) helping a lot of children in Bangladesh through my own foundation; (2) motivating others in get

138

involved in politics and civic affairs; and (3) being a consultant to governments and businesses to enhance the future of the people in Southeast Asia. With all these good efforts going on, I'm sure I will have the enjoyment of even greater respect from my professors when I visit with them again in the future years.

CHAPTER 10

MY ASSOCIATION WITH MORSHED ALAM

by
Chet Szarejko
Chair, Polish American Congress
Former Democratic Party Queens District Leader

For 10 years prior to meeting Morshed, I had been the Democratic district leader for the 24th Summit District in Queens County. While a district leader, I had a full-time job as a social studies teacher in Great Neck High School, Great Neck, New York. Also, I managed a 2,000-member community center. Naturally a community center of that size drew the attention of politicians who came to me for my support.

I became involved politically when I organized members for a Democratic club. Over the years, I developed a very substantial program. One of our clubs, Eastern Queens Democratic Club, became one of the most powerful and strongest Democratic clubs in Queens, as recognized by the county Democratic authorities. Kew Gardens was another key club in the area.

Our club became one of the first to attract a new contingency, that is, we began to get members from the immigrant population representing Southeast Asia, Asia, northern Africa, India, and other ethnic groups. I took an interest in looking for leaders in the ethnic groups in order to

140

expand the ethnic involvement in the Democratic party. Through the Eastern Queens Democratic Club, I met Morshed Alam.

After one of our regular meetings, Morshed and I had a chance to talk. I found myself pleasantly surprised by his eagerness to be involved, his interest in politics, and his concern for humanity. He seemed the epitome of liberalism which I emphasized in my organization.

A new member is highly regarded because new members are very important for any organization to grow. Morshed kept returning to our meetings, and he showed a great interest in our political agenda. He became quite well informed in the political process and began becoming very active in our organization. Morshed was a fairly new immigrant when he came to us. He had already established himself in a responsible position as an employee in a New York City Department of Environmental Protection, was very self-sufficient financially, and had acquired some profitable real estate.

After a while, I said, "This young guy (Morshed) is going places." Since Queens county is such a multi-cultural borough, we were looking for men and women like Morshed who would be active in an election campaign and who could run for office in the future.

During this time, Saul Weprin, a member of our community and the Speaker of the New York State Assembly, passed away. As the Democratic District leader, I was the next in line for the position, if I wanted it. However, I had a variety of other compelling interests that caused me not to run for Weprin's position: my teaching career, managing the community center, and my growing involvement with real estate.

In the meantime, I began to build up my position with a lot of new immigrants. Morshed was a prime example to the others as he became very involved in our Democratic Club: becoming a member of our board of directors; chairman of the board of directors; and playing important roles and positions in advancing the Democratic party.

141

We then approached Morshed to get involved in politics. He began to attend various civic meetings, Democratic meetings, and school board meetings, in an attempt to acquire a positive image. At that time, the way to become a powerhouse politician was to attend every function you could possibly attend and go to every community dinner in order to be seen. One's visibility became paramount in local politics. One had to be at all important political meetings and rallies. The visibility insured credibility.

Morshed became very visible, becoming very well known to other Democratic Clubs and to members of our club. We held him in high esteem and had him featured as a positive member of our community and Democratic party. It appeared he would be ready to run for office. By 1996, he did get elected as a member of a local Queens school board. It typically takes time and a great deal of effort before someone is recognized and can achieve some measure of political success.

His first political goal was to help gather petitions for the different candidates. He went to the candidates' meetings, campaigned on their behalf, and helped in organizing political activities. He worked very extensively with his Bangladesh community and the Southeast Asia community. Petition gathering became very important to the politicians in the area and Morshed proved himself very valuable in this work. People like Morshed were very much needed by the candidates. Morshed and others could establish themselves by following the participatory political routines, learn the parameters of the political nuances, and become well recognized. These procedures could place them into a successful position to become elected officials.

Morshed used his exposure to become an elected school board member and went on to acquire more visibility by helping to organize social and political rallies for himself and for his political allies. Whenever he organized a rally or an activity group, it was heavily attended by politicians. They recognized Morshed as an important and vital political force, because he represented a large number of Southeast Asians in particular. The candidates needed him and his influence to get out the votes and, also, to register new voters.

Morshed became very actively involved with the school board and used that position to further help a wide variety of ethnic groups in his community, especially African-Americans who made up 84% of the population. He always took a very fair approach in supporting different ethnic groups and never said, "I work only for the Bangladeshis." He became a multi-culturalist politically. His whole position philosophically was to serve all groups in his community. I remember from our beginning together that he had always been very community-oriented.

Morshed not only served his immediate community, he came to the Polish-American Congress meetings in Brooklyn to support us. He participated in our club and eventually got an award from the Polish-American Congress for his involvement and help in their community affairs. He pledged his support to the Polish Americans, a new concept in having someone from another ethnicity do that because the Polish American Congress used to be an in-house organization that did not venture out of the confines of the Polish groups.

When I came into the Polish American Congress, I had to broaden their horizons. Morshed became part of the process of helping them get involved with mainstream politics. The Polish American Congress began to develop a power structure which they didn't have before, partially helped by Morshed's influence.

Morshed is determined and willful in that he pursues political initiatives that many of us would ignore. He pursued his dream—to establish himself and other immigrants in American politics. He became very much interested in getting into the Democratic Party leadership of Queens county. The Democratic Party leadership allowed him to participate in state and local Democratic functions. In particular, he was approved to go as an alternate delegate and then as a full delegate to the national convention in 2000 to support Al Gore as president.

Not only did he go, but he also took his daughters with him because he wanted his family to have the same background in political involvement as he had. He upheld the principles of being a good father, a good teacher to other immigrants, and set the standards for people to follow. He pushed his three daughters into positions where they could learn what was taking place and in meeting those who created the power positions and politics of the government, in essence, the shaping of American democracy. I could see the way his children grew and how they came to understand politics and government. I was very proud of Morshed for giving his children the incentive and the background that they needed and that I think is lacking in many American families. I knew that when he ran for office his family would be there to help him in whatever activities they had to fulfill.

By being an accepted member of the larger Democratic community in Queens county, Morshed was able to lend his services and leadership to a variety of positions. The Democratic leaders made him the chairman of the New Americans Committee. It was a natural role for Morshed because he became a leader, not only of his Bangladesh community, but of the whole Southeast Asia communities of Indians, Chinese, Koreans, and others. In addition, he involved himself in the affairs of Egyptians and other Arab Americans. He never showed any discrimination against anyone. That is one of the reasons for his success in the political field.

In 1996, Morshed organized a political club—the New American Democratic Organization of New York. Ninety-five percent of the members were new Americans—both those documented and undocumented. Our position was to help the new Americans to become comfortable with American traditions, to Americanize themselves, and to develop the kind of attitudes that would make them successful.

Our names Chet Szarejko and Morshed Alam started becoming well known as the kind of leaders who were helping new Americans get into the political process and offering them the opportunity to achieve the American Dream. We encouraged the new Americans to join different organizations, become members of the boards of education, go to meetings, go to the PTAs (Parent Teachers Association), join clubs, and to be outspoken.

We were not experts in immigration, so we had immigration lawyers who gave them the information they needed. Although the club became very active, it did gradually dissolve over time as I joined and became a president of a variety of clubs in Queens county. The New American Democratic Club did a great deal of good for a number of years by motivating our members to get involved with the community and adjust better to the American way of life. The rewards of our efforts are proving themselves as we see our members taking their turn to run for office and become district leaders.

Morshed can draw on his great resources of political contacts that he developed during his early period. He now has many followers who look up to him for leadership and to bring out the votes.

With all of Morshed's efforts, the Democratic Party, even today, does not like to have new members who do not conform to their traditional standards. Morshed had experienced rejection from the Democratic leaders because they considered him too much of an ethnic and unwinable. It was quite simply blatant prejudice. In fact, the Democratic leaders were willing to sacrifice Morshed's opportunity to win a state senate seat in order to let Republican State Senator Frank Padavan be re-elected.

A growing number of people became very critical of the Democratic organization and voiced their concerns that the Democratic leaders did not structure their position philosophically for the best interests of their constituents. As a consequence of not having the constituency support, a number of Democrats who ran for office did not get enough votes to get elected. Morshed had by now established enough of a power base to recommend to his followers who should be voted into office. In a curious twist, Monserrate got Morshed's support and became a City Council member against the wishes of the Democratic organization. Hiram Monserrate, a member of the New York City Council from District 21 of Queens became a powerful city councilman, who has support from a Hispanic base where he lives. Whatever office he runs for, he will win automatically, despite the fact that the Democratic Party doesn't like him. Because of Monserrate's power, the Democratic leaders finally became his friends. Monserrate remains a threat to Congressman Joe Crowley. If Monserrate runs for Congress against Joe Crowley, the chances are that Joe Crowley will not win. Crowley does not speak Spanish. He's Irish, while Monserrate is a very suave, sophisticated Hispanic who speaks Spanish beautifully, has a nice personality, and caters to his Hispanic constituency.

At the time that Morshed ran for other elected state offices, he was not accepted by the Democratic Party. Nobody thought that Morshed would run or that he would even win because he had no support from the Democratic organization. He had no money and Frank Padavan was an incumbent powerhouse who had been in office for about 24 years and well liked by the community. In addition, he had secured state money over the years to help his local community.

Frank Padavan felt very secure and had the attitude that nobody could defeat him. He did not bother to run a campaign or do anything special. In slang, we could say he sat on his hands.
Meanwhile, Morshed went out every night after work and knocked on doors. With a very small budget of about $40,000 at that time, he could do very little. If he had the support of the county Democratic organization, he would have won the election. Morshed's election results did have one effect: they ended up terrifying Frank Padavan.

Morshed ran a campaign that gave him a great deal of visibility. Morshed, a young man, nonwhite, Asian, and a new American who had been in the country only a few years, had almost singlehandedly defeated Frank Padavan. That race made Morshed a standard bearer for the new Americans and the immigrants, especially the Asians, who wanted to become Americanized. They said among themselves, "If Morshed can run on a limited budget, why can't I?" Morshed helped to change the direction of politics in New York City. For his efforts, he has accolades from practically every newspaper, politician, and different organizations in the city. By putting out the effort in his political involvement, he now has a great deal of support from different people.

I, also, paid a price when I broke the pattern of loyalty. I supported

146

somebody I shouldn't have. The attitude of the leadership has been, "You support our candidate or you're finished." It did not matter that I had been a district leader for 20 years. I was dispensable when I chose to support a different Democratic candidate. To appease me, I was offered opportunities to move into other jobs with different authorities. However, I never wanted a political appointment because I wanted to stay in my two fields: real estate and teaching.

Morshed did try to run against Frank Padavan a second time. Again, the Democratic machine did not support him. Without that support, Morshed did not have enough money. Without money, no one can continue a campaign. It turned out that another Democrat won that race and is now a State Assemblyman.

1999-2000: An International Agenda

Although Morshed had a great deal of experience in American politics, he never lost contact with the political and business leaders in his home country. In fact, Morshed had a great number of visitors from Bangladesh, people who were commissioners, heads of departments, ministers of agencies, and very prestigious people. As his friend, I had the pleasure of meeting with them and some I took to my home in Southampton, Long Island.

Meeting his country's leaders gave me a new awareness of the leadership of Southeast Asia. Those he introduced me to respected the fact that Morshed and I had been involved with helping the Bangladeshi people here in New York City and had worked mutually to advance their cause.

One of the visitors, Abdur Razzak, the Minister of Water Resources, and I became very friendly. He had been important in his country prior to his present position because he had been a leader and organizer in the Bangladesh war of Independence. As we enjoyed our time together in the Hamptons, we talked about how the United States could help the Bangladeshi people.

Because of my involvement with the Bangladeshi community in New

York City, I was very surprised, but pleased to get an invitation to go to Bangladesh as a guest of the government. So, Morshed and I happily accepted the invitation and we flew to Bangladesh.

We began our stay stayed at a hotel in Dhaka, the Bangladesh capital, for several days. I had the pleasure of meeting with the Prime Minister and the Foreign Affairs Minister. I had the honor of being interviewed with the Foreign Affairs Minister on a half-hour television show to discuss international issues.

It was my pleasure to meet with many prominent people. I also attended Parliament, where my host, Abdur Razzak made a presentation about the economics of Bangladesh and the world economy.

When not meeting with people, Morshed and I toured Dhaka and the environs with the help of a chauffeur. We visited an ancient site, estimated to be about 2,000 years old, about thirty miles outside of Dhaka. The site consisted of the remains of an old university and I was told that this university was the center of Southeast Asia. There was no doubt that this was an impressive historic relic.

Then we visited Morshed's high school. I walked into the classrooms, which were empty at the time, and found myself surprised as to their austerity—wooden benches and limited chalkboards. Out of this austerity, I realized they managed to educate brilliant people—chemists, doctors, lawyers, and leaders of government. The Bangladesh education system differed dramatically from the American schools where I worked which had a host of books and teaching aids.

We took time to tour the district villages and even took an airplane flight to a jungle area where the elephants and tigers still roamed. Where we went we managed time to meet with a variety of officials. On another excursion, we toured the south of Bangladesh to visit the waterfront areas of cities and where I was very impressed with the wonderful beaches at the Bay of Bengal.

I was impressed all during the trip with the kind of people who showed the dedication and spirit to work hard and to develop themselves. They showed a great deal of pride in the work they did. We got to visit Morshed's ancestral family home in the Hajigonj district, a beautiful place, said to be very famous and part of Comilla. While there, I played with the youngsters, communicating happily with them across our language barrier, and had them pose for photographs. I saw small farm lots where people lived and worked on the small acreage. There were pools used for irrigation, but also used by the children for recreation. As the children swam, I was surprised to see their swimming skills, which were as good as American youngsters who swam in the lakes and rivers of America. Being a swimming coach, I admired their advanced swimming skills which had been developed without any formal teaching.

On another day, we flew to Chittagong, Bangladesh's second largest city and a seaport, and then on to Coxes Bazer, a coastal landmark which has a 100 mile long beach.

The trip had been exciting every day. We were treated like family everywhere and in Dhaka we were treated to a lot of parties. I came back with very positive feelings about the Bangladesh people and the culture. All along the way, I had the pleasure of meeting a lot of government officials, professionals, and business people. My impression was that these were people who exhibited a great deal of intellectual knowledge and were very well informed on a variety of issues.

I had been informed that, for the first time that year, they were producing a sufficient amount of rice. In prior years, the rice had to be imported, a situation similar to Burma (Myanmar) and North Korea. For various reasons, there are millions of people around the world who annually depend upon the United Nations and the United States for help during tragic periods. Bangladesh all too often has had cyclones and floods that would wipe out their rice crop.

I had the opportunity to speak with the Foreign Minister and other government people about the fact that they needed to promote the country.

149

At that time, they did not have a marketing strategy to bring the nation into the public view. Other nations have articles and advertising pages in *The New York Times* and other magazines. I encouraged them to do the same. For example, they have beautiful beaches, which they have not developed. I considered the beaches that I saw very beautiful and prime real estate for resort areas. I expressed my belief that the government should spend some money to develop the recreational and tourist industries.

If anyone asked me my basic impressions, I would say that Bangladesh is a beautiful country, the people are very friendly, and I would recommend others go there.

March 20, 2000

Morshed and I went on a second, more impressive trip to Bangladesh only because we were part of the entourage of President Bill Clinton. As part of his international diplomacy, he visited India, Pakistan, and Bangladesh to help with bilateral talks, meeting with the officials about their trade issues. The governments wanted to enhance the trade policies and reduce the tariffs on their product exports. That was a primary reason President Clinton came to Bangladesh.

Our trip had also included a nice luncheon in the Sheraton International. After that, we met at the Prime Minister's house. He had kindly prepared a banquet made entirely of a variety of American food, but no Bangladesh food.

One evening we enjoyed a formal dinner at the beautiful Presidential Palace that included 150 leaders of the Bangladesh government and business. Morshed and I joined a greeting line where we shook hands with everybody, including President Bill Clinton, four American Congressmen, the Secretary of Commerce, Richard Daley of Chicago, and the Secretary of State, Madeline Albright.

The other thing that impressed me was the kind of reception the people of Bangladesh gave President Clinton. They held up his picture all over the streets. At 4 o'clock in the morning, all of us in the entourage left for the airport and we sped through Dhaka. Incredibly, the streets were lined with hundreds, if not thousands of people. The people saw our cars, but they could not see Clinton. They were still outside waiting for the cavalcade and hoping for a rare glimpse of the president. Morshed and I looked out our car window in amazement at the outpouring of people.

We had about ten miles to drive to get to the airport. As we drove along the highway, we saw thousands and thousands of women walking to the city from the outlying districts. We found out that these women were going to work in the garment factories. They had to walk as much as six miles to get to work. There are as many as 18 million women working in the Bangladesh garment industry. They were making very little money, but the jobs were badly needed.

We had achieved something very unique by being part of President Clinton's team. The people of Bangladesh believe in friendship. They were interested in knowing what they could do for me personally. The Minister of Foreign Affairs, who has since passed away, invited us to his home for dinner, but we had to excuse ourselves because we did not have time. Two different Minister gave us two different parties on different occasions in a Chinese restaurant. Other Ministers were asking me to spend time with them. They all wanted me to feel like I was one of them.

When I met Morshed's friends, I saw that Morshed was highly respected by the people in Bangladesh. There's no doubt in my mind that, if Morshed stayed in Bangladesh, he would have had a very important government position. He was a highly respected individual and wherever he went he was greeted with great deference. People respected him because he had succeeded in America and had been involved in American politics, even becoming a prominent Bangladeshi in New York City.

At one point, Morshed had an offer to be an ambassador of Bangladesh in South America and another offer to be a member of parliament, which could have led to an appointment as a government minister. Morshed refused their kind offers. He told them, "I want it to be in the United States. That is my country. My children have grown up here.

151

There are still some adversity to deal with in Bangladesh, but I do not have the time to do that kind of work." One of the urban issues he was referring to in Bangladesh is that of pollution. In the city there is a pollution problem, but outside the city there is little or no pollution.

Appendix A

Asian E-zine Volume 9, Issue 5, December 2004

Asian Americans Breaking Barriers: the Story of One Who Did— Morshed Alam

BY NUSRAT ALAM

This is about the Asian-American political process, a subject I have been deeply exposed to while growing up with my father, Morshed Alam, who has been very active in politics. I was simply left with no choice other than to realize the potential of my father's struggle.

As Helen Zia describes perfectly in *From Nothing a Consciousness*, "Our campus experiences made it abundantly clear that if Asian Americans were to take our rightful place in American society, we would have to scratch and dig and blast our way in, much as the railroad workers had through the Rockies one hundred years earlier. Few in America, or even in our own communities paid much attention to these young Asian Americans.

I'm sure they desired nothing more than an opportunity to add to the great traditions of this country and become part of it. However, among the separate—and expanding—Asian immigrant groups, the vision of pan-Asian unity was not compelling; survival was their main concern."

There is an explanation for this. They came to this country with little or no money. There is also a culture clash once they first come to this country. They may not always know where to start, and because of the clash discriminated against. Nevertheless, the longer these groups are here and the more they get settled in these conflicts should dissipate, because they are more assimilated.

Historically, Asian Americans have always valued placing a focus on preserving cultural identity, a culture that places strong emphasis on personal and familial success. However, on a pragmatic level, day-to-day worries overwhelmingly centered on the families ability to survive in a new and very unfamiliar world.

Though not obvious by any stretch, this is true even today. For instance, although for a number of reasons it is less difficult to pursue a career in politics today, few Asian Americans realize the need to do so. For some reason, they fail to recognize the need to express a voice or exercise their potential political strength (or power) in order to have their needs and views receive more consideration. This may be the reason why little attention is given to Asian Americans and their causes during campaign seasons and when laws or policies are being placed into effect.

Perhaps we can learn from the lessons of Filipino Americans who defended this country by fighting in World War II. They teach us the true value of citizenship, a value that many American immigrants sought to protect with the ultimate sacrifice, their lives. Needless to say, this right is not always freely granted. In many instances, the right must be earned and, on very rare occasions, given away in lotteries. Notwithstanding citizenship status, we come to the United States to learn how to achieve the very best of human potential.

Manuel Buaker, a soldier in the 1st Infantry during WW II wrote, "We came to the United States to learn the best; But we were barred from the best in your society, we were barred from economic advancement, held to the most menial of jobs; condemned for our dark skins, the light of our high ideals ignored and shunned; We have held to the hope that some day you would know us for what we are."

Filipinos enlisted in the Army despite not being considered, or certainly not treated, as citizens. Moreover, they were under no obligation to help America defend itself, yet they did so courageously because they believed and understood it to be their home. Whether or not they were appreciated was irrelevant; they felt a visceral obligation to protect their country.

In the end, their sacrifices were not without reward. When the First Filipino Infantry were granted citizenship they rejoiced at what this meant. They would now be able to exercise their rights to the fullest. They were now capable of fully participating in the political and economic life in America.

Unfortunately, today most of us take this privilege for granted. Most Americans do not always know, or even care, where their taxes are going. Unless personally affected, we pay little attention to what laws and amendments are being passed, even those that could possibly harm us, such as the U.S. Patriot Act. Possibly with the exception with the last election, a vast majority of people do not register to vote, even if they are eligible.

Thus, the question must be asked: why struggle for such rights if we are not to take advantage of them? Perhaps we are comforted feeling secure in knowing that these rights exist and are available should we need them. It is only when they are in jeopardy or at risk do we—as a people—take action.

Although one could argue that a good percentage of the American population does not care for such things, it is vital for every minority to care. Hypothetically speaking, if there were any Asians in public positions during World War II, there is a good likelihood the whole Japanese Internment might not have even occurred. The government would have had to think twice before taking such harsh and unfair actions.

It's the concept of hegemony that Antonio Gramsci presented: a government can only rule with a combination of coercion and consent. If the people are not satisfied they have the power to rise up, no government, especially a democratic one, would like to risk that. They would feel obligated to appease us in some way to keep us down.

One of the biggest issues non-Asian-Americans have with Asian-Americans is our loyalty to America. Unlike African-Americans, we do not have many predecessors, if any, before us. As new immigrants, we still usually hold very close ties to our native lands and culture. To non-Asian Americans, this can be a possibility of bias. They are in a fear of us devoting ourselves more to our homeland than to America.

That is why the Japanese Internment in the 1940s occurred. The American government believed that the Japanese here might be acting as spies for Japan. It was not until the Chinese Americans and Filipino Americans volunteered to help with the War that they realized that Asian Americans indeed could be loyal to the country in which they live. The Chinese Americans were no longer considered the "Yellow Peril" and the Filipino Americans were no longer looked at as "little brown brothers."

Whether one would like to admit it or not, racism is a big factor in any politics and especially in America where there is such a vast range of ethnicities. As Omi and Winant wrote, "For most of its existence both as European colony and as an independent nation, the U.S. was a racial dictatorship. From 1607 to 1865 - 258 years most non-whites were firmly eliminated from the sphere of politics." Importance must, therefore, be drawn to the fact that this racial dictatorship came to symbolize the U.S. and its political arena.

Even if we are to look at the political make-up today, you can see that the ratio of the minority population we have and the elected public officials in offices today drastically differ. Why is this? A big factor is the lack of support from our own communities. If communities were able to stand together with common ideals, they could accomplish a lot. As the Reverend Al Sharpton says, "The minorities of this city are together the majority of this city."

If minorities voted as a block, we would have an abundance of power, with a real voice to achieve what we want. We would no longer be the subordinates but the power and base of America. No longer would we be the minority, but the majority.

I have not always been very understanding of what my father was doing. As a young girl, I was more concerned with what I wanted, which usually consisted of going to the playground or other such places. My father was not always available to take me on such outings; he was away from home trying to "conquer" something that I had no knowledge of until very recently. I know now, and appreciate, the importance of what he was doing even if it meant missing out on a few extra days at Disney.

He was in fact helping me in the long run by bringing down barriers so when my turn comes, there will be fewer hurdles for me to face.

My father Morshed Alam started his activism in the third grade. People here would think this is a young age to start, but in their reality it was something necessary. At that time, Bangladesh was in a midst of a war with Pakistan. There was a great deal of instability. The Pakistan militia was trying to overrun the government and exercise authority over the people through fear.

He started off as captain of his class in the third grade and went on to become the President of the Student Union. In college, he was even more active by being part of a rebellion, which was trying to eliminate Pakistan's power in the country. Unlike in America, being involved in politics is much more dangerous. You do not have the right to vote in secrecy and your party affiliation means everything about who you are as a person and what ideals you hold. There is no such difference in being a moderate or liberal or conservative within the groups. My father was part of the Awami League, which successfully rid Bangladesh of Pakistan's rule.

Although Morshed would have gotten a great job in Bangladesh (he was very highly connected and educated), he knew that having a life in America would be more stable. There was always the threat of being killed or jailed by the opposing party in our homeland. He first emigrated to the U.S. in 1984. He applied for his citizenship and, upon receiving it in 1989, he became active in politics.

When Morshed felt as though he had a good understanding of American politics, he decided to prove himself and ran for the School Board. Being a father of three, he knew it was important that we received a good education. He campaigned very hard, registered a lot of South Asian voters, and, with the support of his family and few friends, he was able to win the election—and do it with the highest percentage of votes.

This was just one battle of many. Although he won in a primarily minority community, the majority of the board members were black. They were not very appreciative of giving up some of their power, even though it was to another struggling minority. As I know personally, one of my father's close friends and fellow politician, John Liu, had a similar struggle being elected as the first Asian-American to the City Council. What was formerly known as the Black and Hispanic Caucus was changed to the Minority Caucus in order to include Mr. Liu.

My father had to work even harder than the other school board members to prove himself. He was able to install new heating systems in the school district. He proposed the plan to replace the old computers with new ones. He even got Bengali to be taught as a second language in some schools with a high percentage of South Asian students. As for the Muslim community, he was able to add halal entrées to the menu.

Nonetheless, as accomplished as he was, when he wanted to run for State Senate in 1998, the Democratic Club chose not to support him as a newcomer. Without any help from his chosen Democratic Party, he took on Frank Padavan, the Republican incumbent of 28 years. Through his own fundraising, advertising, and door-to-door campaigning, he managed to receive a surprising 42% of the votes. As he put it himself, "We went through hell in this campaign, but reached the finish line with honor."

The main objective for running was not necessarily to win (although that definitely would have been great), but to prove a point. Frank Padavan had taken an anti-immigrant stand and did show respect for the immigrant communities, even though they made up a large segment of his district. My father wanted to send the message that the immigrants had to be respected and they should be respected as a political force. After Padavan realized that he had almost lost to my father, he came to respect my father and even supported him when my father decided to run for City Council. My father had to drop out of the campaign for family reasons. Frank Padavan, after 28 years in office, had been forced by my father's election results to recognize the immigrant population and their needs.

Although my father has not run for any public office in the past four years, he has continued to take a very active role in the political community. Other elected officials realized his potential of getting people to register to vote (especially the immigrants) and he was appointed by a unanimous vote on November 20, 2002 to be Voter Assistance Commissioner. He also founded the New American Democratic Club with other members of different ethnicities. The club reaches out to the various immigrant communities in order to educate the new Americans about getting involved in political and civic organizations. Getting people involved has been his one main goals as an activist.

My father is Asian-American. He is a ground breaker and has accomplished so much being the first South Asian-American to win any elected positions in New York City. He has over a hundred plaques and certificates of recognition for his political and civic activism. Newspapers have interviewed him often, and he has been in hundreds of articles.

But he feels all his activism and achievements mean nothing if the younger generations of minority immigrants do not follow his lead. As he states in one interview, "they understand the system better than the first generation like me. We have a language and cultural barrier. But the young don't have that barrier. So it is important for us to encourage them to be active everywhere in the school and in the mainstream." He also believes education is the way to achieve social improvements by helping both the immigrants as to their rights and the established American citizens to respect the new place immigrants have in American society.

To conclude, I am glad to have Morshed Alam as a father. I appreciate that I have not grown to be like countless others, including some of my friends whose parents have shied away from community involvement. As a second generation Asian American, I am trying to follow my father's example and be involved, while knowing that I may not have to face all the barriers my father has faced.

In previous elections, I have motivated many of my friends to volunteer to promote those candidates who want to help the immigrants. Currently, I am working for (AA)2 AURA and the E-zine, Asian American based groups to get a message out. And I am a member of SBU's only sorority, Epsilon Sigma Phi, whose foundation is multiculturalism.

Changes are being made and people are realizing what they have to do. Just in the recent elections, APIA (Asian Pacific Islander Americans) have been responsible for getting many registered in order to show their power through voting. There are other groups, such as 80-20, that tries to get Asian Americans to vote together as a block. If we continue to do what we are doing and become more active in the future, we should someday soon have a governor or mayor of Asian descent.

And who knows, possibly an Asian American President.

ADDENDUM: January 2004 article with a humorous bit on Alam in *The Washington Post*
http://media.washingtonpost.com/ac2/wp-dyn/A57572-2004Jan5?
language=palm&vendor=avantgo
"The college had an annual sports event at the stadium every fall. Even though I am not a sportsman, I put my name as a competitor on all the events: soccer, running, long jump, gymnastics. At the start of each event, they called the names of participants to come to the field while 2,000 students sat watching in the stands. When they called Morshed Alam on the loudspeaker, I didn't come. They announced my name again, Morshed Alam. I still didn't come. By the time they announced my name six times . . . everybody was wondering and looking, who is this guy Morshed Alam? That's when I ran onto the field. I did this for 10 different events. I wasn't good at any of the games, but by the end of the weekend everybody knew my name."

Newsday - New York Hero
http://www.nynewsday.com/features/custom/heroes/newyork/
ny-ehalam051902.htmlstory

Appendix B

Sample of Various Television Interviews

NY1 cable
Interviews about the school board, council elections, and other issues

WNBC
Interviews about the New York State Senate election

Channel 12
Interviews about politics and other issues (Long Island)

Queens Cable Vision
Interviews about political issues

U. S. State Department Documentary television program for Indonesian
TV network

India TV networks
Interviews about immigrants, United States, politics, and other issues

NTV, Channel 1 & ATN TV network for Bengali viewers

Appendix C

Morshed Alam Referenced in Books

Silent No More
by Congressman Paul Findley
photo of Morshed Alam on page 218
reference pages 227-230
Amana Publications

Crossing the Boulevard
by Warren Lehrer & Judith Sloan
"The New American Democratic Club"
photo of Morshed Alam
photo of Saleha Alam (wife)
reference on page 367
W. W. Norton & Co. Inc. (New York City)

Becoming American, Being Indian: *An Immigrant Community in New York City*
by Madhulika S. Khandelwal
see Index: Morshed Alam
Cornell University Press

Distinguishing Awards & Citations

1994
March 20th
Declared as Bangladesh Independence Day
By Mario Cuomo, Governor of New York State

1996
August
Eastern Queens Democratic Club Award For Organizing Democrats in Queens

1997

January
Award from Local Union 375 LPAC

January 19th
Citation by Councilman Sheldon Leffler

April
Award from Probini Foundation—Friends of Community

May 22nd
One of Seven Honorees—Asian-American Heritage Month
Award of Excellence
Presented by New York State Governor George Pataki & ABC, Inc.
(television)

September 23rd
Award presented by Ruth W. Messinger, Borough President of Manhattan

Empire State of Excellence Award
Governor George Pataki of New York State

Outstanding Citizenship: City Council Citation
Sheldon Leffler, New York City Council Member

1998
February 1st
Organizing New Americans into Civic & Political Process
Presented by Assemblyman William Scarborough

June
Award of Education Excellence
By "You Go To School" Community

2000
February
Certificate of Appreciation
By Filipino Chamber of Commerce

Nominated to apply to Rockefeller Foundation
Application to: Next Generation Leadership program (NGL)

2002
May
Outstanding Leadership to Labor Movement
By Asian Heritage Committee of DC-37 AFC-CIO

October
For Outstanding Service & Political Activism
American Federation of Muslims of Indian Origin (AFMI)

October 26
Dedicated Service to Education to Children in the Community
PTA of P.S. 131

October 31
Outstanding Service to the Community
By School Board Member #29

November 4
Certificate of Honor
For Service to Community School Board 29
By Malcolm A. Smith
New York State Senate 10th District

November 4
Applauded for Outstanding Work on Ten Years of Distinguished Service
By Congressman Gregory W. Meeks
U.S. House of Representatives

November 4
Citation Honor to Morshed Alam on His Resignation from Community
School Board 29
By Ada L. Smith
New York State Senate 12th District

November
Outstanding Service to the Community
By City Council Proclamation

November
Dedicated Service to the Education of All Children of Queens School
Board #29
By Michel Johnson, Superintendent

2003
January 6
For Furthering the Interest of Polish American Congress and Their
Community
By Polish-American Congress Downstate New York Division

April 1
For His Contribution As a Tireless Advocate & True Benefactor for
Thousands of Immigrants Across the City
City Council Proclamation
By John Liu, David Weprin & Leroy Comrie
New York City Council Members

May
For Vast Contribution to the Various Ethnic Communities for Queens
County Democratic Organization
City Council Proclamation
By Honorable Councilman Hiram Monserrate

For Selfless Community Service
By Chanpur Foundation Inc., New York

June 1
For Helping the Cultural Advancement of Bangladesh Community
By Udichi USA Chapter

2004
May 19
Commendation for Distinguished Leadership in Service
For His Commitment to Encourage Immigrants of All Ethnic Backgrounds
to Vote and Voice Their Political Opinions
By Honorable Bill Thompson
Comptroller of New York City

June 18
City Council Citation as Outstanding Citizenship
By Leroy Comrie, City Council Member

June 18
Certificate of Recognition For Work on District 29 Queens Community
School Board
By Michael R. Bloomberg, Mayor

June 18
Certificate of Recognition
By Senator Malcolm A. Smith
New York State Senate 14th District

June 30
Certificate of Merit
By Senator George Onorato
New York State Senate 12th District

June 30
Honorable Certificate
By Senator Toby Stavisky
New York State Senate

June 30
Salute to New Americans
By Congressman Anthony D. Weiner
The House of Representatives
United States Congress

July 11
Award for Empowering New Americans in New York State
By South Asian Americans, Club of North Americans

2005

Outstanding Achievement and Public Service to the City of New York
Public Service Award for Career Civil Service Employees
By The Hundred Year Association of New York
(A prestigious award granted to career employees who have distinguished
    themselves consistently in New York City government.)

January 25
Citizen of Distinction
By Helen M. Marshall, President of the Borough of Queens

ADDITIONAL AWARDS AND CERTIFICATES HAVE BEEN
PRESENTED BY

Local 375 of DC-37 AFL-CIO

Congressman Gary Ackerman

City Councilman Sheldon Leffler

New York State Assemblyman Mark Weprin

Figure 1 1992. Morshed and Sheik Hasina, Former Prime Minister of Bangladesh, attending the Democratic National Convention (DNC) in New York City.

Figure 2   1992. Former NYC Mayor David Dinkins, Sheik Hasina, and Morshed in Madison Square Garden for the DNC.

Figure 3 1992. Morshed and his wife, Saleha, with the New York State Speaker Saul Weprin at the State Assembly in Albany, NY at a meeting about immigration rights.

Figure 4 January, 1993. Morshed attending the presidential ceremony as a guest of President Clinton when he took office.

Figure 5   1993. Morshed at a fundraiser for Governor Mario Cuomo in Chinatown, New York City.

Figure 6   1993. Morshed, second from right, the Vice President of the Asian American Democratic Club, with all the leaders of the Asian communities in Queens, NY for a club fundraiser.

Figure 7   1995.   Morshed at the DNC Caucus in Washington, D.C. with the Democratic Treasurer and President Clinton's Chief of Staff.

Figure 8   1996   Left to right.   Congressman Gary L. Ackerman, Bangladeshi Minister Abdur Razzak, and Morshed lobbying for Bangladesh garments and other issues in Washington, D.C.

Figure 9   1996 Left to right. Queens Borough, NYC President Helen Marshall, State Comptroller Carl McCall, Morshed, and State Senator Toby Stavisky.

Figure 10   1996.   Morshed with his family as the New York State Governor George Pataki (Republican) gives him an Award of Excellence for his community service.

Figure 11 1997. Morshed speaking about education at the Spelling Bee Contest for South-Asian children in Floral Park, NY.

Figure 12 1998. Volunteers of the American Bangladesh Friendship Association, with Morshed as the Founder and President, are seen walking down the streets of NYC helping to register voters.

Figure 13 1998. Morshed being interviewed by Channel 13 while campaigning in Queens for the State Senate.

Figure 14 August 18, 1998. Morshed engaged in an election debate with his Republican opponent NYS Senator Frank Padavan.

176

Figure 15   Morshed Alam with New York State Governor Mario Cuomo and Asian-American leaders in NYC.

Figure 16   1999.   Morshed (second from right) standing with Chet Szarejko and the Asian-American School Board members.

Figure 17 1999. Morshed with Dr. Aminul Islam, who gained international recognition as a trade unionist for trying to help Bangladesh workers.

Figure 18 1999. Eastern Queens Democratic Club meeting. Left to right: Morshed, Chief of Eastern Queens Democratic Club; Chet Szarejko, the District Leader; and Louise Marbeck, President of the Eastern Queens Democratic Club.

Figure 19   1999. Vice President and Presidential Candidate Al Gore with Morshed in Queens, NYC.

Figure 20 2000. Minorities Are Majority in NYC Population Seminar hosted by Chamber of Commerce. Speakers were Morshed (far left), Hon. Congressman Charles Rangel (next to Morshed), and John Liu (second from right).

Figure 21   2000. Morshed as the Democratic National Convention Delegate in Los Angeles.

Figure 22 2000. Gary Locke, the first-elected Asian American Governor of Washington State, speaking with Morshed at the Democratic National Convention.

Figure 23   2000. Morshed seated in his Delegate chair at the Democratic National Convention in Los Angeles.

Figure 24   2000. Morshed with his three daughters in front of the Los Angeles Staples Center where the Democratic National Convention was held. Morshed was the first Bangladeshi Delegate.

Figure 25 2000. Morshed and family with former NYC Mayor David Dinkins at the DNC in Los Angeles.

Figure 26 2000. Morshed and Saleha with AFSCME President Gerald McEntee at the convention. (AFSCME stands for American Federation of State and County Municipal Employees)

Figure 27 2000. Morshed with AFL-CIO National President John Sweeney at the DNC.

Figure 28   2000. Left to right: Morshed, Chet Szerajko, and Mr. Abdur Razzak, the Awami League Leader of Bangladesh, at Morshed's Campaign Dinner party.

Figure 29 March, 2000. Morshed with President Clinton and President and former Chief Justice Shahabuddin Ahmed at the Bangladesh Bhaban (The Presidential Palace) during President Clinton's visit to Bangladesh.

Figure 30 March, 2000. Morshed with President Clinton and President and former Chief Justice Shahabuddin Ahmed at the Bangladesh Bhaban (The Presidential Palace) during President Clinton's visit to Bangladesh.

Figure 31 **Morshed and family at a New American Democratic Club Awards Dinner.**

Figure 32 2001. Community Activist Thelma Prescot with Morshed's wife and daughters at a School Board reception for Morshed.

Figure 33   2001. The late Spiritual Leader Sri Chinmoy blessing Morshed Alam.

Figure 34 2001. Morshed with Mayor Michael Bloomberg at the mayor's inauguration at the NYC City Hall.

Figure 35   2002. Morshed with his fellow Trade Union activists at DC37 Union and Local375 AFL-CIO during the NYC May Day procession.

Figure 36 Morshed with Mrs. Tipper Gore, wife of Vice President Al Gore, and NY State Senator Malcolm Smith.

Figure 37 2002. Chet Szarejko, Morshed, and Congressman Gary Ackerman at a fundraising dinner for Senator Hillary Clinton.

Figure 38 October, 2002. Morshed receiving appointment as Voter Assistance Commissioner from New York State Speaker at NY City Hall.

Figure 39 Morshed and Saleh with famous Bangladesh columnist Abdul Guffer Chowdhury and Samuel I. Alamzir, a famous photographer, at a reception for them in Queens, NYC.

Figure 40 Morshed with DNC Chairman Howard Dean.

Figure 41 January 6, 2003 Morshed with Chet Szarejko and the Polish students where Morshed was given an award by the Polish community.

Figure 42 2003. Morshed with Democratic Presidential Candidate General Clark.

Figure 43 2003. Reception for Morshed for his appointment as Voting ssistance Commissioner.

Figure 44 2005. Keynote Speaker Morshed Alam on the "American Election Mechanism" in Dhaka, Bangladesh with Former Foreign Minster Dr. Kamal Hossain, Former Commerce of Industries Minister Tofaiel Ahmed, Mission Chief USAID Mr. Gene George, and Mr. M.E. Chowdhury Shameem, Founder &

President   of Scholars Bangladesh.

191

Figure 45 2006. Left to right: NY State Senator Frank Padavan (Republican) and Mayor Bloomberg with Morshed at the NYC Memorial Day parade.

October 18th, 1997

Figure 46 October 18, 1997. Newsday newspaper political cartoon.

ABOUT THE AUTHOR

Morshed Alam was born and raised in Bangladesh. During his high school years, he acted as a courier for the Bangladesh Freedom Fighters who finally secured Bangladesh freedom from Pakistan. He has a B.S. and master's of science degree from the University of Dhaka, Bangladesh. He and his wife emigrated to the United States in 1984, where he worked as a chemist. He became a United States citizen and considers America his beloved home. Since 1992, he has worked for the New York City Department of Environmental Protection. He was twice elected to School Board 29 in Queens; founded the New American Democratic Association; became executive director of the Bangladesh American Friendship Association; and ran for the New York State Senate, which showed the power of the immigrant community when he obtained 42% of the vote. He has been the recipient of numerous civic awards for his contributions to the school board and the immigrant community. One of his honors was being invited to accompany President Bill Clinton on his trip to visit the South Asian countries of India, Bangladesh, and Pakistan. The New York City Council has recognized his community involvement by voting him to be a Voter Assistance Commissioner. He and his wife have three daughters, and his family has been involved with him in his campaigns and civic causes. One of his recent projects is to help establish a medical clinic and education scholarships for the people in his home village. He looks forward to working with the South Asian countries to establish new business ties with American businesses in order to help South Asia to continue to prosper.

Donald MacLaren has worked as an editor for Morshed Alam on his book. He lives and works in Tampa, Florida (formerly in New York City 18 years) as a ghostwriter, editor, and co-author on book and movie projects. He can be reached at donmac100@gmail.com and by telephone: (813) 252-6279 (direct) or 718-932-7720 (cell).